# MANAGING INTERNATIONAL ASSIGNMENTS

## The Strategy for Success

Gary Fontaine

Department of Communication
University of Hawaii

Prentice Hall
Englewood Cliffs, New Jersey 07632

**Library of Congress Cataloging-in-Publication Data**

Fontaine, Gary.
  Managing international assignments.

  Bibliography: p.
    Includes index.
    1. Americans—Employment—Foreign countries.
  2. Corporations, American—Personnel management.
  I. Title.
  HF5549.5.E45F66 1989 658'.049 88-32205
  ISBN 0-13-551904-7

Editorial/production supervision
  and interior design: **Jacqueline A. Jeglinski**
Cover Design: **Wanda Lubelska Design**
Manufacturing buyer: **Mary Ann Gloriande**

© 1989 by Prentice-Hall, Inc.
A division of Simon & Schuster
Englewood Cliffs, New Jersey 07632

The publisher offers discounts on this book when ordered
in bulk quantities. For more information, write:
    Special Sales/College Marketing
    Prentice-Hall, Inc.
    College Technical and Reference Division
    Englewood Cliffs, NJ 07632

Printed in the United States of America
10 9 8 7 6 5 4 3 2 1

ISBN 0-13-551904-7

Prentice-Hall International (UK) Limited, *London*
Prentice-Hall of Australia Pty. Limited, *Sydney*
Prentice-Hall Canada Inc., *Toronto*
Prentice-Hall Hispanoamericana, S.A., *Mexico*
Prentice-Hall of India Private Limited, *New Delhi*
Prentice-Hall of Japan, Inc., *Tokyo*
Simon & Schuster Asia Pte. Ltd., *Singapore*
Editora Prentice-Hall do Brasil, Ltda., *Rio de Janeiro*

To Mom, Dad, Lorna, Renato, and Wellyn

# CONTENTS

PREFACE

**CHAPTER 1**     INTRODUCTION                                    **1**

    An International World     2
    International Assignments     3
    The Ecology of International Assignments     6
        *Ecological Similarities*     6
        *Ecological Differences*     8
        *Task-Specific Characteristics*     10
    An Overview of the Book     12
        *The Themes*     12
        *The Objective*     13
        *The Foci*     14
    A Final Note     15


**CHAPTER 2**     DOING BUSINESS AT HOME          **16**

    Perception     17
    Convergence and Communication     21
    Culture     22
    The Ecological Basis of Culture     23
    Levels of Culture     25
        *National Culture*     25
        *Organizational Culture*     31
    Some Final Notes     37


**CHAPTER 3**     MICROCULTURES                        **39**

    MCs     40
    Some Related Approaches     42

Characteristics of Specific MCs     49
Manipulating the Task Ecology     52
A Final Note     54


**CHAPTER 4**     DOING BUSINESS
INTERNATIONALLY     **55**


Coping with Ecoshock     57
    *The Symptoms of Ecoshock*     58
    *The Phases of Adjustment*     60
    *Reentry*     64
Doing Business Effectively     66
    *Commonly Described Orientations*     66
    *What Must Actually Happen*     72
A Final Note     77


**CHAPTER 5**     INTERNATIONAL
MICROCULTURES     **79**


IMCs     80
Some Related Approaches     83
    *Expected Behaviors*     84
    *Strategic Responses*     85
Characteristics of Specific IMCs     85
    *The Task Ecology*     86
    *The Lifetime of an IMC*     92
    *The Members of an IMC*     93
How Specific IMCs Are Developed     94
The Quality of an IMC     97
Skills in Developing IMCs     98
Some Final Notes     99


**CHAPTER 6**     A SENSE OF PRESENCE     **102**


A Perceptual Skill     103
The Necessary     108

The Possible    111
The Desirable    111
Some Related Approaches    114
    *Stereotyping*    114
    *Attributions*    116
    *Empathy*    117
    *Generic Problem Solving*    118
Some Final Notes    120

## CHAPTER 7    SOCIAL, COMMUNICATION, AND STRESS-MANAGEMENT SKILLS    **122**

Social Skills    123
Communication Skills    126
    *Information Exchange and Social
        Influence*    126
    *Matching Language*    128
    *Matching Ritual*    129
    *Perspective Sharing*    130
    *Matching Agendas*    133
    *Presence in Telecommunication*    135
Stress-Management Skills    136
A Final Note    140

## CHAPTER 8    SCREENING, SELF-SELECTION, AND ORIENTATION    **141**

*Management,* Not Just *Training*    142
The Objectives for Managing International
    Assignments    143
A *Management* Strategy    146
A *Generic* Strategy    148
Screening    151
    *Traditional Approaches*    151
    *The Role in Managing International
        Assignments*    153
Self-selection    154

Orientation    155
　　*Traditional Approaches*    156
　　*The Role in Managing International*
　　　*Assignments*    160
A Final Note    162


# CHAPTER 9    TRAINING                      163


Technical or Professional Training    165
Language Training    166
Culture Training    168
　　*Training for a Sense of Presence*    169
　　*Training for Social Skills*    175
　　*Training for Communication Skills*    176
　　*Training for Stress-Management*    178
Other Training Concerns    180
　　*Should Training Be Culture Specific or Culture*
　　　*General?*    180
　　*Who Should Receive Training?*    181
　　*Who Should Provide Training?*    181
　　*What Should Be the Duration of*
　　　*Training?*    181
　　*How Should Training Be Provided?*    181
　　*Where Should Training Take Place?*    181
　　*When Should Training Take Place?*    182
Some Final Notes    182


# CHAPTER 10    ARRANGING TRAVEL,
ACCOMMODATION, AND SUPPORT              184


Travel    185
　　*What Is Jet Lag?*    186
　　*How Can We Cope with Jet Lag?*    188
Accommodation    190
　　*The Role of Hotels in Coping with*
　　　*Ecoshock*    191

*The Role of Hotels in Doing Business
    Effectively*    192
Support    194
    *Organizational Support*    194
    *Social Support*    197
    *IMC Networks*    199
    *Skills in Developing Support*    203
A Final Note    206


**CHAPTER 11**    SOME *FINAL* FINAL NOTES    **207**

A Synopsis    208
Managing Inter*cultural* Assignments    208
Managing Organizational Change    210
*Education,* not Just *Management* or *Training*    213
Reducing Conflict in International Business    213


INDEX    **215**

# PREFACE

Our world has become *international*. To do our business successfully today we must rely *not* on habits developed at home in the past—however effective there—but on strategies responsive to the international world we face. We must do this whether our business is in commerce, diplomacy, science and technology, education, entertainment, tourism, transportation, relief or refugee programs, religion, communications, or the military. And to do business internationally typically requires *going there,* be it a short-term assignment to negotiate a treaty or a long-term one to manage a subsidiary.

This book provides both practical and conceptual guidance into the management of these international *assignments.* It provides an honest, realistic assessment of the requirements for doing business consistently effectively on them and what personnel and their organization can do to maximize that opportunity. It reviews the commonly described strategies for doing business internationally and their weaknesses. It describes an optimal strategy for doing it and the essential skills associated with this strategy. The book then shows how an organization can best *manage* programs for screening, self-selection, orientation, training, travel, accommodation, and support to help personnel in using that strategy.

The book is useful as a *companion guide* for personnel in preparation for and during their international assignments; as a key *source* for managers, trainers, and human resource specialists responsible for organizational programs to manage these personnel; and as a *textbook* for students in academic or professional programs in international management, international relations, international studies, intercultural and international communication, or human resource development. Because it concisely reviews much of the current theory and research in the field and goes on to make substantive original contributions, it is intended also as a *resource* for the researcher and consultant.

The book fills a large gap between material currently available focused primarily on *comparative* management and *cross-cultural* training ("how other cultures do business") and the full requirements of *managing international assignments* ("how to do business with other cultures"). Issues are presented within an integrated theoretical perspective yet are illustrated at a very practical level. The focus is *international*—on personnel from any country assigned to any country.

In writing this book I owe much to those who have had a major impact on either the general perspective or the specific ideas presented in it. They include Richard Brislin, Carlos Castaneda, Norm Dinges, Bob Hayles, Fritz Heider, Reed Maurer, Sandy Mumford-Fowler, Ken Sanborn, Harry Triandis, and Art Whatley. In some instances they labored through early versions of the manuscript; in others their input came through conversations or seminars. In no case, however, should they be held accountable for what I've done with their ideas. I thank my family, friends, students, clients, and colleagues who provided support yet understood my need for distance during preparation of the manuscript and Susan Shinogi and the "Elves" for the countless little things required in that preparation. Finally, I would like to give a special thanks to the many people throughout the world who have shared their work and their lives with me—however briefly—and taught me so much.

Honolulu, 1988

# INTRODUCTION

Chapter 1

# AN INTERNATIONAL WORLD

**Our world has become international.** Whether our portion of that world lies in commerce, diplomacy, science and technology, education, entertainment, tourism, transportation, relief or refugee programs, religion, communications, or the military, it too is international. No longer is international activity the domain solely of career diplomats, missionaries, or adventurous import/export traders. That's the most dramatic fact closing this century: the world is no longer *becoming* international—it *is*!

This fact is well documented in several recent publications.[1-6] From 1948 through 1984, world exports grew from US$ 51.4 billion to US$ 1.9 trillion.[7] For the United States alone exports of goods and services rose from US$ 65.7 billion in 1970 to US$ 358.5 billion in 1985.[8] Similar statistics illustrate the vast increase in international diplomatic activity.[9,10] That activi-

1. Adler, N. (1986). *International dimensions of organizational behavior.* Boston: Wadsworth.

2. Chesanow, N. (1985). *The world class executive: how to do business like a pro around the world.* New York: Rawson Associates.

3. Copeland, L. & Griggs, L. (1985). *Going international: how to make friends and deal effectively in the global marketplace.* New York: Random House.

4. Desatnick, R. L. & Bennett, M. L. (1977). *Human resource management in the multinational company.* New York: Nichols.

5. Globerman, S. (1986). *Fundamentals of international business management.* New York: Prentice-Hall.

6. Harris, P. R. & Moran, R. T. (1979). *Managing cultural differences.* Houston: Gulf.

7. 1983/84 Statistical Yearbook (1986). New York: United Nations.

8. Statistical Abstract of the U.S. (1987). U.S. Department of Commerce.

9. Winham, G. R. (1977). Complexity in international negotiation. In Druckman, D. (Ed.), *Negotiation: Social psychological perspectives.* Beverly Hills: Sage.

10. Zartman, I. W. & Berman, M. R. (1982). *The practical negotiator.* New Haven: Yale University Press.

ty is no longer restricted to the relatively infrequent negotiation of defense treaties or trade agreements but is now involved in even the most mundane tasks required for nations to live together such as the regulation of air and water pollution and airline traffic and the control of drugs. Not only is the frequency of diplomatic activity increasing dramatically, but so too is the number of nations participating in that activity. Similarly, foreign students and faculty are major components of university campuses throughout the world; the international tour can be a "pot of gold" for the entertainer and a requirement for world-class status as an athlete, and on and on.

For many of us, the most significant part of our world is **doing business internationally.** The term "doing business" here and throughout this book is used in the sense of "getting the job done" or "completing the tasks required" to meet the objectives of *any type* of organization. Meaning is *not* restricted to the world of commerce. While "doing business" internationally is often critical in commercial organizations, it is by no means limited to them, as we shall see shortly. Throughout this book, examples are drawn from a range of organizational types, and, unless otherwise stated, it is assumed that the issues exemplified in one have relevance to all.

## INTERNATIONAL ASSIGNMENTS

The amount of travel associated with doing business internationally has increased along with the increased importance and frequency of that business. The number of international passengers carried by the world's airlines rose from 73.7 million in 1970 to 180.8 million in 1984.[11] Americans alone make over 5 million international business trips a year, and the median annual cost of that travel per firm has risen to US$ 557,000.[12] Individual per diem rates in major cities are commonly in the US$ 175 to US$ 200 range. At the same time, there has been a vast increase in funds expended to both develop and distribute new telecommunication technology to meet the information requirements of doing inter-

---

11. 1983/84 Statistical Yearbook. (1986).

12. Copeland & Griggs (1985). *Going international.*

national business when face-to-face contact is unnecessary, excessively expensive, or impractical.[13]

But most of us *know* all this. Even if we are unfamiliar with the latest statistics, we know the role we, our organization, or our clients play in it. We know it because we or they are there. Or we are trying to get there. The point of departure for this book is that *doing business internationally most typically requires going there to do it successfully*: "going there" both in the sense of short-term assignments to develop a contact or negotiate a treaty and in the sense of long-term assignments to monitor a project or manage a subsidiary. We must go there because our organization, clients, and competition are there.

The term "international assignment" is used throughout this book as a shorthand way of referring to travel to another nation to do the business of an organization. Although an increasing amount of international business can be completed with the use of modern telecommunications, these alternative means are not a replacement for face-to-face interaction in today's highly competitive international world.

Use of the term "assignment" is not limited to those cases in which personnel are literally given an order with specific objectives by organizational superiors. It also includes cases where persons are doing business on their own and are themselves responsible for setting the objectives. Further, much of what is said about these assignments is applicable to those not doing business for an organization at all but traveling internationally for personal goals: doing the "business" of a tourist, a vacationer, or a sojourner. All these roles also involve tasks that need be completed to do them successfully. The focus here, however, is on assignments as they exist *within an organization for organizationally defined objectives*.

The impact of international assignments on personnel adjustment and effectiveness is readily documentable and, for many organizations, painfully obvious. Up to 60 percent of all international assignments end in premature return or unacceptably poor performance; over 10,000 Americans return early each year with

---

13. Rahim, S. A. & Wedemeyer, D. J. (1983). *Telecom Pacific*. Honolulu: University of Hawaii Press.

direct costs of such returns running up to US$ 200,000 per employee.[14] That totals to an impressive US$ 2 billion a year in direct costs. The indirect costs of poor performance in terms of lost treaties, contracts, and sales; damaged reputations; unrealized profit expectations; failed mergers, join ventures, and acquisitions; and attrition of good managers are inestimatable.[15,16] Certainly failure to handle these assignments adequately is one of the major factors influencing an organization's lack of international success.

Few personnel sent overseas, or the managers responsible for them, receive any special training. They must rely on their previously developed skills and experience. *Sometimes* they succeed. But business experience in one's home culture is not a guarantee of success elsewhere. Estimates are that only 20 percent of American personnel sent overseas without special training do well. Their failure to perform adequately can have a severe impact on organizational effectiveness: only 1 in 25 negotiations with Japan succeed.[17] Even the most "nuts and bolts" businessperson finds that, internationally, the metric used (and that's a lot more than language!) is different. If we try to force the bolt, try to do it our way, often all we achieve is simply "stripping the threads"—and the contract, the treaty, or the productivity of an international subsidiary is lost!

**The world is international.** Only the people and organizations that recognize and deal effectively with this fact are going to be successful. We can no longer depend on the skills developed in our own culture to be effective with others. Business is *not* the same everywhere! Management, supervision, marketing, negotiation, decision making, planning, training, performance appraisal, communication, and even the meaning of "success" are different. And the management of those on international assignments must be different, too.

14. Copeland & Griggs (1985). *Going international.*

15. Desatnick & Bennett (1977). *Human resource.*

16. Ricks, D. A., Fu, M. Y. C. & Arpan, J. S. (1974). *International business blunders.* Grid, Inc. 1974.

17. Copeland & Griggs (1985). *Going international.*

# THE ECOLOGY OF INTERNATIONAL ASSIGNMENTS

The **ecology** of an international assignment consists of the physical, biological, and social environment in which tasks on that assignment are completed. The ecology might involve, for instance, the characteristics of the facility in which a task is completed, the health and safety conditions of that facility, and the skills, expectations, and status relationships of the task participants, respectively. There are characteristics of the ecology that are commonly *similar* across different assignments and that distinguish them from their domestic counterparts. Likewise, there are characteristics of the ecology which frequently *differ* between assignments and set one international assignment apart from others.

### Ecological Similarities

It is those characteristics that are relatively similar across assignments that allow us to talk about "international assignments" in the first place, and the explication of them defines what such assignments are. If there were no similarities, we would be forced to treat each assignment solely as a unique combination of ecological characteristics with nothing about *management* to be learned from one about another. While each of the following ecological characteristics may vary somewhat between international assignments, it is their relative consistency compared to domestic assignments that is the concern here.

*Place.*    International assignments take place in another nation, often at a considerable distance from home, with a different climate and topography, at perhaps a different time of day or season or no obvious "season" at all. We are not at home, and that, if nothing else, makes them psychologically different from domestic assignments. Singapore is a long way geographically, topographically, climatically, and psychologically from Denver.

*Time.*    It generally takes longer to "get things done" on an international assignment, yet because of the expenses involved, there is often a greater pressure to minimize the time. "Deadlines" take on a special emphasis because of the common perception that "this is our only chance, we will be leaving tomorrow, and we won't be meeting again!"

*Travel.*   To get to the international assignment site, we must travel. The preparation, time, and stress associated with it are usually much greater than on domestic assignments. Travel is an event in itself—on short-term international assignments, it may be the major event. A business trip to South America to meet with agents marketing our product involves coping with numerous visas, immigration and customs officials, often tiring flights, and jet lag.

*Communication.*   Distance, time-zone disparities, and media unreliability can make communication with the home office difficult at a time when, because of the unpredictability of events, good communication is critical. New York and Seoul are 11 time zones apart: it's tough to communicate in "real time," and if we do, somebody is half asleep. Communication with *host* country participants can be difficult for many reasons, and interpreters may be required. Even if all speak a common language, it is rarely the primary language of all. In meeting with ASEAN representatives in Kuala Lumpur, we may find that English is spoken by all—but probably not *our* English.

*People.*   Participants are usually from different national and organizational *cultures*. They look, live, dress, eat, and do business differently. They have a different government and that government may have a very different orientation to our business. They have a different educational system and philosophy. They have different union and work force attitudes. They have different laws. They have different technologies. The impact of these differences is certainly one of the most noted characteristics of international assignments.

*Support.*   An international assignment produces disruption of social and organizational support at the time they are most needed. We are taken out of that nurturing environment we all need to be consistently effective. Most of us give very little thought at home to the pervasiveness of our support structure. The inability to fill these needs adequately abroad can be, and often is, what brings us home early. In Saudi Arabia our wife may not get along with the expatriate community and find few others to whom to turn; we may find the home office unsympathetic with our inability to meet their deadlines.

**Structure.** "Here I am, now what do I do? Where do I start?" At home assignments are usually well, and repetitiously, structured: when we get off the plane for a domestic assignment, we know what we must do, who we must see, and the sequence. Internationally assignments are much less structured: we may may not know what, who, or when! Once we unpack our luggage *we*—not our boss or family—must figure out what to do next, sometimes for months. We need to take the initiative.

### Ecological Differences

There are also characteristics of international assignments that distinguish one from another. They are what give a specific assignment a unique flavor and what make preparation for such an assignment so difficult. Doing business as an American diplomat in Geneva is different from doing business as a Dutch businessman in Jakarta. While assignments are ecologically similar because they involve doing business with *people* different from those at home, the specific people involved provide much of the unique character of an assignment—this includes the characteristics of the *traveler* in terms of culture, age, language skills, and degree of international experience. The same can be said about a specific *place*, or type of *support*, and so forth. Some other important distinguishing characteristics are presented in the paragraphs that follow.

**Type of Organization.** An illustrative list of organizational types that commonly involve international assignments includes commercial, diplomatic, military, intelligence, advising, consulting, transportation, educational, humanitarian, goodwill exchange, scientific, news, communications, athletic, entertainment, religious, refugee, tourist, and recreation. Obviously the international assignment of a diplomat can be quite different from that of an international volunteer health worker.

**Locus of Organizational Identity.** Organizations differ in the extent to which they identify themselves as a *national organization* (based in one country but doing business internationally), a *multinational organization* (based in one country with international components, but centralized control and perspective and one-way movement of personnel), or a *global organization* (characterized by decentralized control, a global perspective, and worldwide exchanges of personnel). With General Motors, for instance, the technology division seems national, the automotive division multinational, and the component division more global. These identities produce quite different characters to the assignment ecology.

*Face-to-Face Versus Mediated Interaction.*    Doing international business effectively usually requires going there for face-to-face interaction. Setting up a subsidiary, negotiating a contract, supervising a project, or meeting clients requires a smile, bow, or handshake and a close eye on what's happening. However, some tasks can be completed via post or telecommunications: setting the agenda for a future visit to a branch office in Great Britain or arranging a symposium of scientists in Geneva could be done by teleconferencing. Each medium has its own ecological character in terms of speed, clarity, feedback, social presence, and the skills required to use them effectively.

*Short- Versus Long-Term Assignments.*    Assignments vary from short to long term with different impact on social and organizational support requirements, concern with travel and accommodation, and the time available for programs associated with the management of an assignment such as screening and training. *Short term* and *long term* tend to be defined relative to what is typical for a particular organization. Commonly, however, a short assignment is anything from a few days to two years; a long assignment is two to five years. If we've been there longer than five years we call it "home."

*A Bilateral Versus Multilateral Context.*    More and more international business is being conducted between participants from *several*, rather than just two, nations. The added complexities in terms of cultural and communication differences can profoundly affect the assignment ecology. The United Nations is no longer the only multilateral forum. There has been poliferation of a vast array of regional and global associations requiring multilateral exchange in military, trade, health, scientific, athletic, and many other contexts.

*A Cosmopolitan Versus Provincial Destination.*   There are major ecological differences between assignment to destinations with a large international community and a high level of international business activity versus those with no international community and a low level of international business activity. Doing business in Los Angeles, Paris, Hong Kong, or Mexico City is not the same as doing it in Spokane, Rangoon, or St. Vincent.

*Differences in Technology.*   The challenge of doing business on an international assignment is increased if faced with technology that is different or simply less developed. If our way of doing that business depends on a particular technology, doing it that way can be alternatively obsolete or impossible.

*Giving Versus Exchanging Versus Getting Roles.*   There are major differences in ecological character among assignments in a **giving role** (giving knowledge, technology, or resources to a host culture requesting it), or an **exchanging role** (exchanging knowledge, technology, or resources with a host culture when both parties gain through the exchange), or a **getting role** (obtaining needed knowledge, technology, or resources from the host culture). Foreign study, for example, involves "getting," providing advice on telecommunications technology involves "giving," negotiating a treaty involves "exchanging." These roles involve differences in social power that affect the perceived need, and subsequent motivation, of participants to accommodate each other's objectives, constraints, and ways of doing business. At a more subtle level, however, *all* forms of international interaction most likely involve some—if often disguised—exchange.

## Task-Specific Characteristics

Within any given assignment there are **task-specific ecological characteristics** that differentiate the ecology of each task on an assignment from others on that same assignment. These include the task objectives; the importance of those objectives; the physical setting in which the task takes place; the resources available; the degree to which the task is structured; the number of participants, their past experience with one another, their current relationships, their anticipation of future interaction, and their motives, skills, and personalities. The number of potentially relevant characteristics is vast and depends on the kind of task involved: riding a taxi, negotiating a treaty, marketing a new product, conducting a seminar, or entertaining guests. As we will see in the following chapters, an appreciation of both ecological similarities and differences as well as these task-specific characteristics is critical to doing international business effectively. They are all depicted in summary form in Figure 1.1.

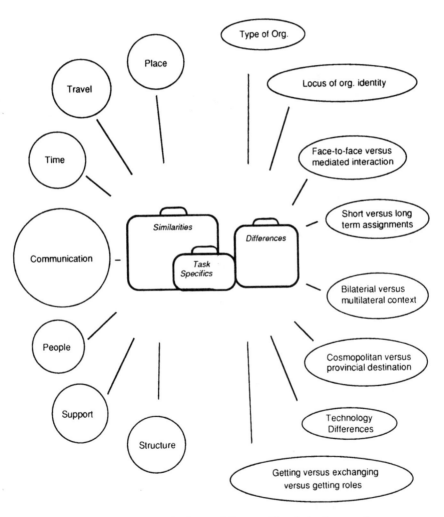

**Figure 1.1**   The Ecology of International Assignments

# AN OVERVIEW OF THE BOOK

## The Themes

In the past two decades we have seen a rapid expansion of cross-cultural training programs. Most commonly these programs teach us how to understand better other cultures and how they do business. The basic premise has been: "If we're going to do business with the Chinese (or Japanese, or French, or Americans, or whomever), we must learn to do business their way, so we can do it their way or at least compromise." But the way people do business with one another in their own culture is not necessarily the way they would do it with us. Cross-cultural training tells us what someone from another culture is *used to* thinking and doing—and perhaps what he or she is *good at*—but not necessarily what he or she *expects* or will *think* or *do* in interaction with us!

When we do business with internationally sophisticated Koreans (or whomever), they won't expect us to do it their way. With rare exceptions we never could. It has taken a *career* for *them* to learn to do it their way. We are not going to learn in a one-week or one-year training program. To attempt to do business their way will be viewed by them humorously, at best, or more likely as evidence of our own *lack* of international sophistication.

No, what those experienced in doing business internationally must learn is that to do such business effectively requires the skill to build **international microcultures** quickly within which they and their hosts can negotiate, make decisions, manage, supervise, and communicate. As we will see shortly, these are ways of doing business tailored to the ecologies of the specific tasks associated with an international assignment. *Without them, international business does not get done well or simply does not get done at all!*

\*That is the FIRST THEME of this book.\*

The key skill in developing international microcultures is a **sense of presence**: an ecological awareness of the characteristics of place, time, travel, communication, people, support, structure, the characteristics that differentiate assignments from one another, and the characteristics of the specific tasks that must be completed as part of an assignment. *It is a sense of the* *necessary, the possible, and the desirable in specific tasks.* It is the international assignment equivalent of "street smarts."

*That is the SECOND THEME of this book.*

Also important are the **social skills** to develop and maintain international relationships, **communication skills** to maximize understanding, and **stress-management skills** to help moderate the often high levels of stress experienced on assignments. Together all four of these skills represent an interrelated "package" critical to the development of international microcultures and assignment success.

The foregoing skills are the basis for an *inter*cultural, as opposed to *cross*-cultural, approach to doing business internationally: learning "how to do business with other cultures" *rather than* "how other cultures do business." Simple awareness of—or training in—these skills, however, does not at all assure that those on a given international assignment will have them. That assurance requires the proper management of *all* organizational **programs** relevant to an international assignment. These programs include screening; self-selection; orientation; training; and arranging travel, accommodation, and support. Thus the successful international assignment must be *managed* in a manner focused on the requirements for developing international microcultures!

*That is the THIRD THEME of this book.*

This book first presents approaches to the description of how business is done at home and the role of microcultures in that process. It then examines the challenges of doing business internationally in terms of **coping with the ecoshock** commonly produced by assignments and **developing strategies to do business effectively in assignment ecologies.** It then directly addresses all three themes: the characteristics of international microcultures, the skills for developing them, and the consequent requirements for managing international assignments.

### The Objective

The objective of this book is to provide both *practical* and *conceptual guidance* into the management of international assignments. This insight is essential for those participating in such assignments (both the assigned personnel and their hosts), the organizational staff responsible for preparing them (managers, trainers, human resource development specialists), and those studying their effectiveness (students, professors, researchers, consultants). In most good programs today they all work together and must continue to do so for the foreseeable future: there simply is not a "working technology" for managing assignments that "professionals" can turnover to "practitioners" and walk away from. Perhaps there never will be. They all must work together, study the issues together, and speak the same language. Thus this book is intended for them all. Material in the book is usually presented from the perspective of the person on assignment ("We on assignment . . .") because I feel they are the easiest for all the interested parties to relate to.

The authors of most books directed at those on international assignments make the assumption that they cannot—or at least do not wish to or have the time to—*think*. These authors appear to assume that assignment participants simply want to get to the "bottom line." Sorry, but in terms of how best to do business internationally, *the bottom line is that there is no bottom line!* That, of course, is part of the whole problem. Right from the very beginning I offer this advice: *those who can deal only with a bottom line, best stay home.* This book is for thinking participants and those preparing or studying them. It may at times seem directed most at a social scientist. In a sense it is. We need to be participant-scientists to do international business successfully. Those without an inquiring mind, who must be given an invariable recipe, may sometimes succeed at home—internationally they *rarely* do.

### The Foci

This book is focused on the management of both *short- and long-term international assignments*. The focus is *not* limited to participants from any specific country or those assigned to any specific country. It is for all those involved in assignments from "wherever" to "wherever." Much of the documentation presented concerns participants *from* North America and Europe, but that is simply because more data on them are available. Many of the illustrations are taken from assignments *to* the Asia/Pacific region, but that is simply because this has been the source of much of my own experience.

The book is focused principally on assignments in the *exchange* role (doing business within joint ventures or multinationals, negotiating contracts and treaties among participants aware that both have much to gain and lose) as opposed to giving or getting roles. Managing these assignments is most complex because the relatively equal distribution of power makes things more uncertain, and the burden of reducing uncertaintly must be *shared* more between participants. It also is the context that increasingly typifies contemporary international business as more and more nations and organizations better understand their own resources, resource needs, and mutual dependence.

Finally, the book is focused principally on *face-to-face* rather than *mediated* assignments. This is because for the foreseeable future such a context will be most important. I do not, however, intend to neglect the rapidly expanding role of international telecommunications, and that context is addressed at select points. With these qualifications, this book addresses issues relevant to the full range of international assignments important in today's world.

## A FINAL NOTE

Throughout the book case illustrations are used to provide clarity to the topics presented. Although for the most part based on real cases, they have been modified to varying degrees to highlight the topic of concern, to disguise the identities of some or all the real participants (who otherwise might be either pleased or displeased, but certainly surprised, to see their assignments in print!); or both. This license is taken because the cases are not used to support the points made, as a case study might, but simply to illustrate them. I'm confident that readers with any international experience will find themselves quickly illustrating the points with cases of their own as well.

# DOING BUSINESS AT HOME

# Chapter 2

The first step in understanding how to do business successfully internationally is to examine how we typically do it that way at home. At home we negotiate a contract, conduct a meeting, develop a friendship, resolve a conflict, hire, supervise, train, reward, delegate, communicate, or buy a bag of potatoes as our culture teaches us within a *familiar* ecology. *Our culture specifies how we do business.* This point is not novel, of course, and is a central perspective in contemporary management.[1,2] But to understand the process by which it occurs, we must examine the interactive relationships between perception, convergence, communication, culture, and ecology described in this chapter. These relationships are depicted in summary form in Figure 2.1.

## PERCEPTION

**Perception** is the process by which we define, give meaning to, interpret, or make sense out of the world around us. More explicitly, it is the process by which we place *stimuli* in *categories* on *dimensions* of meaning important to the task at hand: Is a person happy or sad, attractive or unattractive, talented or untalented, a good or bad employee? Is a contract fair or unfair, firm or negotiable? Is a conflict necessary or avoidable? Is consensus valued? And so forth. Once we have categorized all the important stimuli in an environment (an office, a classroom, our home, or the freeway), we have established the *reality* of that environment. Once we have done that for all the environments we encounter, we have established the reality of the world in which we live.[3,4]

1. Conrad, C. (1985). *Strategic organizational communication: Cultures, situations, and adaptation.* New York: Holt, Rinehart and Winston.

2. Hofstede, G. (1984). *Culture's consequences: International differences in work-related values.* Beverly Hills, CA: Sage.

3. Singer, M. R. (1987). *Intercultural communication: A perceptual approach.* Englewood Cliffs, NJ: Prentice Hall.

4. Triandis, H. C. (1972). *The analysis of subjective culture.* New York: John Wiley.

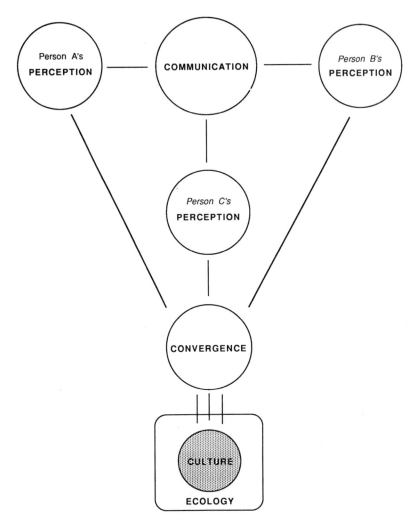

**Figure 2.1** How We Do Business

The importance of this perceptual process shouldn't be underestimated. We do it to understand our world better so that we can predict and interact effectively with it: so we can *do business* successfully. If our perceptions of how to do business are appropriate, we do it well, we survive, and we are happy and productive. Without them we would be naked, vulnerable, and ineffective; there would be no sense to the world; and our success in it would be based on luck or the benevolence of others. We must understand this from the very beginning: *we defend our perceptions, including those about how to do business, with vigor.* We do not give them up easily. We probably would be crazy to do so!

So where do our perceptions come from? How do we know which dimensions and categories to use? How do we know attractiveness is important? Or intelligence? Or productivity? How do we know *who* is attractive, *who* is intelligent, or *what* productivity means? How do we know what makes a good leader, how to conduct a meeting, how to discipline, how to plan, how to delegate, what should be in a year-end report? How do we know what skills are important and how they should be taught? How do we know the proper way to communicate? The answer is that these perceptions are the "gift" of our culture. They come from our parents, peers, and siblings; from teachers, preachers, therapists, bosses, and bar hostesses; from television, films, books, magazines, and newspapers. *They come from our communication networks—our culture.* Since we all have a unique set of networks, we all have somewhat different perceptions of the world and how to do business in it.

We can, of course, ignore the messages of these others or filter them or synthesize them. We can apply them to our own personal world in different ways. We can, in other words, *think* for ourselves. This will differentiate our perceptions somewhat from those in our networks. Ironically, it may produce some convergence with those in *other* networks. Thus both a Muslim Palistinian male and a Jewish Israeli male may see a role of women in conflict resolution that neither's network would propagate because they both understand curfews: women are allowed out to buy food (and communicate), men are not. We are all "thinkers," but we share much with those with whom we live and work. Those shared perceptions can be called our **subjective culture.**[5]

Since our perceptions come largely from our culture, then of course people raised in different cultures have different perceptions. They place more or less importance on attractiveness, love, happiness, productivity, achievement, cooperation, status, harmony, directness, and efficiency and will define them all differently. They live in different realities; *they do business differently.* If they come from very different cultures, they may do it *very* differently.

---

5. Ibid.

We usually behave as though the world exists "out there" for everybody to see and the way we see it is the *way it is*; that there is a "right way" to do business, for everybody. From this viewpoint those whose perceptions differ from us are wrong, backward, or crazy. Others have "myths," we have "truth." But our reality is *relative* to the culture in which we live and do business, it exists in our minds. At home many perceptions may be *universal* (we all see things about the same), but that does not make them *absolute*. Somebody tomorrow could see things differently—on an international assignment they probably will!

The relativity of our perceptions for how to do business is easy to understand and accept intellectually. Those with much international experience probably do. But, as we will see, it is very difficult to *believe* in our heart or liver or wherever our culture says the "center of us" is. For most, a significant encounter with another culture is the first time we must seriously confront it.

To see more clearly the very practical nature of perception and how it relates to doing business, I suggest the following exercise.

## Exercise

Get some paper and a pen, and select a person for examination. Anybody around will do. OK, what do you see? Start with the basics: Who is "that"? A man? A woman? List all the terms you would use to describe the person. Take your time. When you seem to be stretching it, stop.

Look at your list. It represents your *perception* of one small part of your reality: one stimulus, a person. What *categories* did you use to make sense out of it? The categories are the terms you listed. What *dimensions* of perception do each of these categories represent? For example, if the category is "woman," the dimension is "gender." What did you notice first? What were the most important dimensions to you? What were least important? What cues did you use to place the person in specific categories along the dimensions? That is, how did you determine it was a woman? Or old? Or intelligent? Or attractive? Or well organized? Or whatever?

Try it with another person. Again, look at your list. What dimensions did you use? Did the same ones emerge? If so, they may be key dimensions that you use to perceive people generally.

Try it again with another type of stimulus: your relationship with a subordinate, the day at the office, a contract or treaty you are negotiating. With the latter, what is the "proper" way to do it? That is, how do you perceive you should go about negotiating it? What is the objective? What is "fair"? Who should be involved? How long should it take? And so on. Make your own list of what you perceive about doing the business of negotiating.

Your perceptions are the categories you used within dimensions of importance to you. You sum all them together and you have the meaning of the world to you, the reality you live in, how you expect to go about doing business at home!

In the preceding exercise, note that *everyone* would describe that same person or negotiation differently. If you don't believe it, ask some others to do the same thing. Compare lists. No two people in your office or the world will see the same thing. The reality of that person or that task is different to everyone. Ours will be more similar to some (those sharing a subjective culture with us) than to others, but it won't be the same as anybody else's. And nobody is right or wrong—we just see the person or the task differently.

That is what perception and doing business are all about. I suggest applying it to the range of issues related to international assignments addressed in this book. There is probably *nothing* more important to keep in mind on those assignments, themselves. Our reality is just that—ours! And everyone, particularly those from different cultures, will always have another. The goal is not just to understand this point, but to do business that way.

## CONVERGENCE AND COMMUNICATION

Since we all perceive how to do business somewhat differently, some **convergence** in our perceptions must occur for us to do business effectively with one another. We must come to agreements on the appropriate way to do business *together*. We thus become more similar to one another in at least those perceptions about how to do the task. For some tasks the **tolerance limits** (the perceptual diversity allowable) are quite broad: negotiating a diplomatic treaty requires convergence on relatively few aspects of reality, not on religion, child rearing, cooking, or who should take out the garbage. For other tasks the limits might be much more narrow: a marriage may require convergence on all these. And it's important to note that as this convergence occurs, we are *diverging* from those not participating in the task with us.[6] We must converge with people to do business and we must diverge from them when it's finished so we can move on.

**Communication** facilitates convergence by helping us to understand better the perceptions of those with whom we are working.[7,8] The content of what we communicate is our perceptions related to the task: what we think of that person, or this role, or some problem. We generally do not try to communicate our *whole* reality (only after work in intimate discussions over many beers!). Communication and perception are thus related in that communication with others in our networks *forms* our perceptions and our perceptions are *what* we communicate to them. Further, many of our perceptions are related to how best to communicate and thus guide the *style* we use to do it.

Both differences in perception and in communication cause problems when doing business at home. As we will see in Chapter 4, a major challenge of doing business internationally is that we and our hosts are starting out farther apart in perceptions and the chief tool for converging—communication—is more difficult.

## CULTURE

Convergence and divergence in perceptions aided by communication is the process by which we form and change **cultures**. Thus a culture is not a static thing lying out in the world for us to observe or to put in a museum to preserve, though we may try to. A culture is a growing, changing, dynamic thing consisting most significantly of shared perceptions in the minds of its members.

---

6. Barnett, G. A., & Kincaid, D. L. (1983). Cultural convergence: A mathematical theory. In W. B. Gudykunst, (Ed.), *Intercultural communications theory: Current perspectives.* Beverly Hills, CA: Sage.

7. Ibid.

8. Cronen, V. E., & Shuter, R. (1983). Forming intercultural bonds. In W. B. Gudykunst, (Ed.), *Intercultural communications theory: Current perspectives.* Beverly Hills, CA: Sage.

It is a shared way of looking at the world and, as a consequence, doing business in it. It is passed from older to newer members, from one generation to another, through people and institutions. It is formed and continuously changed by the tasks necessary for living and working in it and the people communicating to complete those tasks.

Culture is defined, then, as **shared perceptions**, not by ethnicity or race or nationality. That sharing may stem from common experience produced by ethnicity or nationality, but it could also stem from *any* common experience: being in a profession, working for an organization, playing for a team. And it's important to keep in mind that the sharing is never total. We never share everything. But the more widely a perception is shared by others, the more cultural it is. What distinguishes a "cultural" difference from an "individual" difference is *the degree to which we believe that our perceptions are shared by others.* The more we believe it, the greater our expectation that others will agree with us, the greater our confidence in our correctness, and the greater our surprise when our perceptions are not validated—it's not just *my* way of doing business, it's *our* way! And if we perceive ourselves to be powerful, we'll generally perceive our culture to be best.

## THE ECOLOGICAL BASIS OF CULTURE

We should ask again: Where do the shared perceptions come from? We saw that one answer is that they come from communication with others in our culture. But why do *they* look at the world, or how to do business in it, the way they do? Why do business this way and not some other? The answer is that the **ecology** of the tasks we must complete to live and work determines which perceptions are more appropriate to completing those tasks successfully. The ecology (the physical, biological, and social environment) within which we exist is most significantly the basis of our culture.[9,10]

The ecology does not *determine* which specific perceptions are held; it determines the *parameters* within which some perceptions

9. Berry, J. W. (1975). Ecology, cultural adaptation, and psychological differentiation: Traditional patterning and acculturative stress. In R. W. Brislin et al. (Eds.), *Cross-cultural perspectives on learning.* New York: John Wiley.

10. Dawson, J. L. M. (1969). Research and theoretical bases of bio-social psychology. *Gazette, 16*(2). 1–10.

are likely to be more useful than others. Traffic conditions in Hong Kong or parking restrictions in Singapore make stress on strict punctuality a useless perception for business meetings. The breadth of the parameters is influenced in part by the *severity of the environment* and *the degree of technological control* we have over it. Just what technology does, of course, is to alter the severity.[11] For example, in a severely cold or hot environment there simply is not a great deal of selection in what we can wear. The appropriateness of wearing fur coats in Darwin or shorts in a Moscow winter are not likely to be widely shared perceptions because they would interfere with successful completion of some important tasks. In a more moderate climate, both might be appropriate. But technology can turn a severe climate into a moderate one: air conditioning in Darwin; heat in Moscow!

An appreciation of the ecological basis of culture is important because it allows us to see why a person or culture looks at the world, the organization, or a task they way they do. Their perceptions, though often different from our own, become understandable. They make sense. We see that these people are not ignorant, backward, or crazy, but do business the way they do because of the task ecologies they face.

This appreciation generally makes differences between them and us less threatening. Their perceptions, while valid in their world, do not delegitimize our own for ours. Different cultures developed in different ecologies can both be effective (legitimate). Further, even different perceptions developed in relatively similar ecologies can be effective as long as the ecological parameters are not too narrow. Only when the parameters are very restrictive should differences become threatening because they suggest that somebody's perceptions are "wrong."

An appreciation of the ecological basis of perception is even more important because of its implications for how *we* should perceive a task. Should we retain our perception and do the task our way, change our perception to theirs and do it their way, or attempt to change their perception to ours? For example, in making a decision should we do it "democratically" and force a vote, should we cautiously exchange viewpoints and develop a "consen-

---

11. Ibid.

sus" as they may prefer, or should we convince them of the value of a "vote"? Or should we use our ecological assessment to develop some alternative way to do the task that is responsive both to their perceptions and ours and to other characteristics of the task ecology? Without an ecological assessment we have no rational basis on which to make these decisions. In such a vacuum the decision is often based instead on who has the most power. As we will see shortly, an ecological assessment is the key to doing business effectively both at home and internationally.

## LEVELS OF CULTURE

Culture can be manifested at a *national* or *macro* level in which perceptions are broadly shared by people of a nation or ethnic group or profession (American, Chinese, or medical culture, for instance). At this level the culture is often institutionalized in laws, regulations, and customs that transcend many generations. Culture can also be manifested at the level of *organizations* within which perceptions are shared by organization members (a company, a hospital, a federal department, a football team, a family). At this level culture is often formalized in policies and procedures and lasts for the lifetime of the organization. Finally, culture can be manifested at a *micro* level in which the sharing may be limited only to those participating in particular occurrences of specific tasks and is limited to the duration of the tasks themselves. At this level, culture is not frequently institutionalized, formalized, or even recorded.

The remainder of this chapter looks at the roles of national and organizational culture in doing business at home. As we will see, however, both domestically and internationally *it is most significantly at the micro level that business actually gets done.* Examination of this level is initiated in the next chapter.

### National Culture

An early and continuing concern in international management has focused on **national culture.** The primary objective has been to define the perceptions shared by members of a particular country and which best differentiate them from those of other countries. A brief list is presented here. It is only a sample. There is a rapidly growing literature describing a larger range in much more detail.[12-15] In reviewing this or other lists, it is important to keep in mind that in no case would everyone in a particular country perceive something in the manner described. There can be as much within culture variation as between. But we can usefully expect that certain perceptions will be more widely shared one place than another and that we should be *prepared* to encounter them.

- A perception of people and nature as independent and in a competitive relationship with one another versus interdependent—with implications for the perception of the value of technology.
- A belief in an ability to control the environment versus fatalism—with implications for planning, decision making, and problem solving.
- An emphasis on analytical versus intuitive or holistic understanding—with implications for research, education, and training.
- A materialistic perspective with a value placed on quantity versus a more spiritual, sensual, or experiential one with a value placed on quality.
- A value placed on doing versus belonging—with associated differences in values placed on equality, membership, status, and age.
- A belief in limited versus unlimited distribution of resources—with implications for sharing, hoarding, cooperation, and competition.
- A belief in individual versus communal ownership of property—with implications for the distribution of the benefits of that property.

12. Adler, N. (1986). *International dimensions of organizational behavior.* Boston: Kent.

13. Chesanow, N. (1985). *The world class executive: How to do business like a pro around the world.* New York: Rawson Associates.

14. Harris, P. R., & Moran, R. T. (1987). *Managing cultural differences.* Houston: Gulf.

15. Stewart, E. C. (1972). *American cultural patterns.* Chicago: Intercultural Press.

- A past versus present versus future orientation—with implications for the value of planning, progress, change, tradition, and continuity.
- A preference for monochronic (doing things sequentially) versus polychronic activity (doing them simultaneously)—with implications for scheduling and meeting dynamics.
- Differences in the perception of time—with implications for punctuality, deadlines, and efficiency.
- The individual or self versus the relationship, family, or community as the primary unit of value—with implications for the value of independence, self-reliance, collectivism, dependence, freedom, and authority.
- A value on honesty versus harmony in relationships—with implications for directness and indirectness in communication.
- Differences in the degree of formality expected in relationships.
- Differences in role expectations in relationships and the objectives of the relationships, themselves—with implications for rights, responsibilities, and relationship stability.
- Differences in forming, maintaining, and dissolving relationships.
- Differences in both verbal and nonverbal communication symbols, languages, styles, and strategies.

Another way to phrase the opening of this chapter is that an important first step in understanding how to do business internationally is to understand better *our perceptions at home* along the dimensions just illustrated. What is the cultural basis of how we do business in our own country? Again to give some of the perceptions more concrete relevance, I suggest the following exercise.

## Exercise

Imagine that your ship has just sunk. Your group is safe on a raft with a good chance to survive. There is still room for *three* more people. Make a choice from the accompanying list below of the three persons you would take on board.

A 10-year old child
An injured woman
A 30-year-old man
A married couple in their seventies
A medical doctor
A religious leader
A ship's officer
A newly wed couple

List the perceptual dimensions you used in *differentiating among the persons* to make your selection; for example, "survivability," "ability to provide assistance," or "most likely to benefit from a longer life." Identify the perceptions (or categories within each dimension) that led each person to be selected or excluded.

This list represents some of your perceptions or values appropriate to this task. How cultural are they? Do you feel that they are consistent with most others in your culture? If you're not sure, try it. Have some other people make their selections and discuss among yourselves the bases of those selections. Which perceptions seem broadly shared? Which do not? The more broadly shared perceptions are likely to be part of your shared national culture.

If possible try the exercise with a culturally diverse group and see what you get. Try to see if the group can arrive at some consensus in their selection. Looking ahead to subsequent chapters, observe the problems that occur in the process of negotiating a consensus in this intercultural context and the strategy used to deal with those problems. How effective was the strategy? That is, did you get a consensus with which everyone was satisfied?

The list of perceptions shared at the national level potentially related to doing business is too large to be of much practical use. At a minimum, what is needed is some grouping of them. To meet that need, Hofstede differentiates four dimensions of "work-related values" based on a study of employees in international offices of a large U.S. multinational.[16] The dimensions are described next, with the mean score on each for the countries studied presented in Table 2.1.

- **Power distance** involves the distribution of social power in the organization is reflectedin the structure of authority. Hofstede defines it as the difference between the extent to which the boss can determine the behavior of the subordinate and the subordinate can determine the behavior of the boss. For example, in a *high-power-distance* country bosses exert much more power in decision making than their subordinates; in a *low-power-distance* country power over decisions is more equally distributed.

- **Uncertainty avoidance** is associated with the need to control, plan, and proscribe as well as with rigidity, dogmatism, and intolerance for ambiguity and differing opinions. It is reflected in the structuring of activities rather than authority. For example, in a *high-uncertainty-avoidance* country, managers are typically selected on seniority; in a *low-uncertainty-avoidance* country, performance criteria are more commonly used.

- **Individualism** involves concern with individual versus collective values in the organization and is positively associated with stress placed by the organization on personal time, freedom, individual challenge, training, the opportunity to use skills, and working conditions. For example, in *high-individualism* countries managers rate autonomy as important; in *low-individualism* countries security is more important.

- **Masculinity** reflects an achievement orientation and the centrality of work in employee's lives versus a social orientation with work less central. It is positively associated with the work goals of challenge, advancement, recognition, and earnings and negatively associated with the desirability of good relations with the manager, cooperation, a desirable area to live, and employment security.

---

16. Hofstede. *Culture's consequences.*

For example, in *high-masculinity* countries, company intrusion in workers' lives is accepted; in *low-masculinity* countries such interference is not.

**TABLE 2.1**  Mean Scores on Work-Related Perceptual Dimensions*

| Power Distance | | Uncertainty Avoidance | | Individualism | | Masculinity | |
|---|---|---|---|---|---|---|---|
| Philippines | 94 | Greece | 112 | United States | 91 | Japan | 95 |
| Mexico | 81 | Portugal | 104 | Australia | 90 | Austria | 79 |
| Venezuela | 73 | Belgium | 94 | Great Britain | 89 | Venezuela | 73 |
| India | 77 | Japan | 92 | Canada | 80 | Italy | 70 |
| Singapore | 74 | Peru | 87 | Netherlands | 80 | Switzerland | 70 |
| Brazil | 69 | France | 86 | New Zealand | 79 | Mexico | 69 |
| Hong Kong | 68 | Chile | 86 | Italy | 76 | Ireland | 68 |
| France | 68 | Spain | 86 | Belgium | 75 | Great Britain | 66 |
| Colombia | 67 | Argentina | 86 | Denmark | 74 | West Germany | 66 |
| Turkey | 66 | Turkey | 85 | Sweden | 71 | Philippines | 64 |
| Belgium | 65 | Mexico | 82 | France | 71 | Columbia | 64 |
| Peru | 64 | Israel | 81 | Ireland | 70 | South Africa | 63 |
| Thailand | 64 | Colombia | 80 | Norway | 69 | United States | 62 |
| Chile | 63 | Venezuela | 76 | Switzerland | 68 | Australia | 61 |
| Portugal | 63 | Brazil | 76 | West Germany | 67 | New Zealand | 58 |
| Greece | 60 | Italy | 75 | South Africa | 65 | Greece | 57 |
| Iran | 58 | Pakistan | 70 | Finland | 63 | Hong Kong | 57 |
| Taiwan | 58 | Austria | 70 | Austria | 55 | Argentina | 56 |
| Spain | 57 | Taiwan | 69 | Israel | 54 | India | 56 |
| Pakistan | 55 | West Germany | 65 | Spain | 51 | Belgium | 54 |
| Japan | 50 | Thailand | 64 | India | 48 | Canada | 52 |
| Italy | 50 | Iran | 59 | Japan | 46 | Pakistan | 50 |
| South Africa | 49 | Finland | 59 | Argentina | 46 | Brazil | 49 |
| Argentina | 49 | Switzerland | 58 | Iran | 41 | Singapore | 48 |
| United States | 40 | Netherlands | 53 | Brazil | 38 | Israel | 47 |
| Canada | 39 | Australia | 51 | Turkey | 37 | Turkey | 45 |
| Netherlands | 38 | Norway | 50 | Greece | 35 | Taiwan | 45 |
| Australia | 36 | South Africa | 49 | Philippines | 32 | Iran | 43 |
| West Germany | 35 | New Zealand | 49 | Mexico | 30 | France | 43 |
| Great Britain | 35 | Canada | 48 | Portugal | 27 | Spain | 42 |
| Switzerland | 34 | United States | 46 | Hong Kong | 25 | Peru | 42 |
| Finland | 33 | Philippines | 44 | Chile | 23 | Thailand | 34 |
| Norway | 31 | India | 40 | Singapore | 20 | Portugal | 31 |
| Sweden | 31 | Great Britain | 35 | Thailand | 20 | Chile | 28 |
| Ireland | 28 | Ireland | 35 | Taiwan | 17 | Finland | 26 |
| New Zealand | 22 | Hong Kong | 29 | Peru | 16 | Denmark | 16 |
| Denmark | 18 | Sweden | 29 | Pakistan | 14 | Netherlands | 14 |
| Israel | 13 | Denmark | 23 | Colombia | 13 | Norway | 8 |
| Austria | 11 | Singapore | 8 | Venezuela | 12 | Sweden | 6 |

*From Geert Hofstede, *Culture's consequences: International differences in work-related values.* Beverly Hills, CA. Copyright © by Sage Publications, Inc., 1984.

Descriptions of countries derived from their rankings along these four dimensions support both popular stereotypes and much current research on differences in national culture: the United States, for instance, can be characterized as being relatively low in uncertainty avoidance and high in individualism. These are certainly four important dimensions at the national level, although they are not necessarily the only, or always the most important, ones. Bond, for example, has recently identified *Confusian work dynamism* as one important dimension in differentiating some Asian countries.[17] Another study examining dimensions similar to the foregoing ones found significant differences between Japanese and Korean managers: both valued materialism, but the Japanese put more emphasis on time, collectivism, uncertainty avoidance, and power than the Koreans.[18]

These findings not withstanding, however, when we take such *general* descriptions of a national culture and ask if they would apply to a *specific* organization, the answer is a frustrating "it depends." *It depends on the organization.* So it is to culture at the organizational level that we now turn.

### Organizational Culture

There is common recognition that within any national culture, organizations can differ considerably in how their people do business. Cultural descriptions at the national level are based largely on observations of frequently shared perceptions at the organizational level. Indeed that's the source of Hofstede's dimensions: descriptions of the values of members of a specific organization in each country. But such descriptions are not necessarily representative of how business is done within other organizations. Thus, much recent concern has focused on what is called **organizational culture.**

Organizational culture involves all aspects of organizational activity, and there is a rapidly expanding literature describing the

---

17. Bond, M. H. (1986). Mutual stereotypes and the facilitation of interactions across cultural lines. *International Journal of Intercultural Relations, 10,* 259–276.

18. Kelley, L., Whatley, A., Worthley, R., & Lie, H. (1986). The role of the ideal organization in comparative management: A cross-cultural perspective of Japan and Korea. *Asia Pacific Journal of Management, 3*(2), 59–75.

important perceptions associated with it.[19,20] As with national culture, the list is too large to be of much practical use. Again, some grouping of the perceptions is necessary. One such grouping, based in part on that of Harris and Moran,[21] is presented here.

- *Communication.* Perceptions associated with the use of professional or other specialized languages, acronyms, forms of address, nonverbal symbols, and specific media. In some companies everyone addresses everyone else by their first name; in other companies their role, title, or last name only is used. Some companies prefer brief exchanges over an intercom; others prefer memos.
- *Appearance.* Customs or rules related to attire and appearance, uniforms, color of clothes, length of skirts, requirements for safety apparatus. Some companies require identical attire; others similar attire; others give very little attention to attire at all.
- *Eating habits.* Differences in what is eaten, when, where, how long, and with whom. In some companies personnel eat only at designated times and places; in other companies personnel are perpetually eating everywhere. Some companies discourage discussing business over meals; in other companies that's where most of the business is done.
- *Time.* the meaning and importance of "punctuality," the unitization of time increments during the day, monochronic versus polychronic scheduling, emphasis on immediate profits versus long-term stability. Some companies are concerned with when personnel "punch-in" and "punch-out"; other companies are concerned primarily with *what* personnel do, not *when* they do it.
- *Rewards.* Means of responding to positive and negative performance in terms of commendations, citations, promotions, raises, pins, ranks, bonuses, cars, stock options, demotions, firings, warnings, and so forth. Some companies promote personnel through a seemingly endless

19. Adler. *International dimensions.*

20. Copeland, L., & Griggs, L. (1985). *Going international: How to make friends and deal effectively in the global marketplace.* New York: Random House.

21. Harris & Moran. *Managing.*

series of levels and grades; others give them a gold watch after 30 years and that's about it. Unions can influence whether such policies are company specific or industry general.

- *Relationships.* Organizational structure, work units (teams, companies, squads), who interact with whom and how, communication networks, sex roles, status and ethnic factors, the role of spouses. Some companies encourage the development of personal relationships between company members; others forbid it—especially between members of different levels. Sometimes the policy extends to those that spouses and children are allowed to socialize with as well. The appropriateness of romantic relationships within the organization is often of particular sensitivity.

- *Values and norms.* Importance and expectations associated with level of effort, doing one'd duty, observing rules, overtime, teamwork, reliability, customer service, and so forth. Sometimes these are formalized in personnel manuals, performance criteria, and union contracts.

- *Management processes.* Perceptions on a broad range of issues associated with management such as decision making, training, leadership, institutional socialization, human resource development, information acquisition, sales, marketing, public relations, negotiation, supervision, planning, policy making, and motivating.

To illustrate how these and other perceptions related to organizational culture affect us and our organization, excerpts from a useful exercise developed by Handy are presented next.[22]

## Exercise

In each of the items listed, the task is to rank from 1 (most preferred) through 4 (least preferred) your own preference for the alter-

---

22. From *Understanding organizations* by Charles Handy (Penguin Books, 1976, 1981). Copyright © by Charles Handy, 1976, 1981.

natives and your perception of your organization's preference (your current company or one that you are considering joining or one with which you may be working on an international assignment).

| *Own Rank* | *Org. Rank* | |
|---|---|---|

**A good boss**

|  |  | is strong, decisive, and firm but fair. He is protective of, generous to, and indulgent of loyal subordinates. |
|---|---|---|
|  |  | is impersonal and correct, avoiding the exercise of his authority for his own advantage. He demands from subordinates only that which is required by the formal system. |
|  |  | is eqalitarian and influenceable in matters concerning the task. He uses his authority to obtain the resources needed to get on with the job. |
|  |  | is concerned and responsive to the personal needs and values of others. He uses his position to provide satisfying and growth-stimulating work opportunities for subordinates. |

**A good subordinate**

|  |  | is compliant, hard-working, and loyal to the interests of her superior. |
|---|---|---|
|  |  | is responsible and reliable, meeting the duties and responsibilities of her job and avoiding actions which surprise or embarrass her superior. |
|  |  | is self-motivated to contribute her best to the task and is open with her ideas and suggestions. She is nevertheless willing to give the lead to |

*Own      Org.*
*Rank     Rank*
_____

others when they show greater expertise or ability.

_____   _____   is vitally interested in the development of her own potentialities and is open to learning and receiving help. She also respects the needs and values of others and is willing to give help and contribute to their development.

A good member of the organization gives first priority to

_____   _____   the personal demands of the boss.

_____   _____   the duties, responsibilities and requirements of his role, and the customary standards of personal behavior.

_____   _____   the requirements of the task for skill, ability, energy, and material resources.

_____   _____   the personal needs of the individual involved.

People who do well in the organization

_____   _____   are shrewd and competitive with a strong drive for power.

_____   _____   are conscientious and responsible with a strong sense of loyalty to the organization.

_____   _____   are technically competent and effective, with a strong commitment to getting the job done.

_____   _____   are effective and competent in personal relationships, with a strong commitment to the growth and development of people.

| *Own Rank* | *Org. Rank* |
| --- | --- |

The organization treats the individual

———————   ———————   as though his time and energy were at the disposal of the persons higher in the hierarchy.

———————   ———————   as though his time and energy were available through a contract having rights and responsibilities on both sides.

———————   ———————   as a co-worker who has committed his skills and abilities to the common cause.

———————   ———————   as an interesting and worthwhile person in his own right.

It is legitimate for one person to control another's activities

———————   ———————   if she has more authority and power in the organization.

———————   ———————   if her role prescribes that she is responsible for directing the other.

———————   ———————   if she has more knowledge relevant to the task at hand.

———————   ———————   if the other accepts that the first person's help or instruction can contribute to the other's learning and growth.

Now take the sum of the *absolute value* (disregard the − sign) of the differences between the rankings on each item. The greater the score, the greater the difference between your perceptions of the way to do business and those of your organization: between your organization's culture and you. The size of the discrepancy is likely to affect your satisfaction, adjustment, and the need for accommodation. The exercise can be more useful still if key organizational executives complete the organizational preference and if your score is compared with that of others.

## SOME FINAL NOTES

Within organizational cultures typically encountered in the United States, studies sponsored by the *American Management Association* and the *Academy of Management* have looked for the skills that differentiate the most "effective" managers from their peers. Studies by the former have identified entrepreneurial, intellectual, socioemotional, and interpersonal skills as key.[23] Studies by the latter have identified communication, human resource management, traditional management, and networking skills—with communication having the strongest relationship to effectiveness.[24] These appear to be the "package" of skills effective American managers possess. At home, what they do well that best differentiates them from others is communicate.

The skills identified above are *generic*; that is, they are the basis of effective management across a range of organizations and tasks. But whether they are also the skills that differentiate effective managers in organizational cultures quite different from those in the United States just isn't known. There is controversy over whether organizational cultures are converging internationally as a product of increased contact.[25] Some evidence suggests that in terms of organizational structures and technologies they are, but that in terms of the perceptions of people within the organizations, they are not.[26] The increasing similarity of organizations in the former, more *visible* characteristics may give the *incorrect* impression that less visible differences in organizational culture are no longer a problem. This mistake may reduce the incentive to develop

23. Hayes J. L. (1980). The AMA model of superior performance. Part II: How can I do a better job as a manager. *Management Review*, February.

24. Whatley, A. (1988). New Mexico State University. Personal communication.

25. Adler, N. *International dimensions.*

26. Child, J. (1981). Culture, contingency, and capitalism in the cross-national study of organizations. In L. L. Cummings and B. M. Staw (Eds.), *Research in organizational behavior*, Vol. 3. Greenwich, CT: JAI Press.

an appreciation of some of the very differences that affect most how the business is done!

Nevertheless, we *never* really do business with a nation *or* an organization. We do business with *specific people* in the *specific tasks* necessary to complete that business successfully. For example, we do not do business with IBM; we do business on specific tasks with specific people in a specific office of IBM. Organizational cultures are in reality nothing but general representations of commonly shared perceptions at the task level. Sometimes the former are truly representative in the sense of being the most common or frequent perceptions occurring at that level; sometimes they are biased toward the outstanding or unusual. When we take these still general descriptions at the organizational level and ask if they would apply to a specific task within the organization, the answer is that still frustrating "it depends." It depends on the task. So we turn next to an examination of the role of microcultures in doing business at home. We will see that it is they that have the most meaningful implications for doing business internationally as well.

# MICROCULTURES

Chapter 3

A **microculture** (MC) is a set of shared perceptions along those dimensions important for doing business on a *particular occurrence* of a task: not, for instance, on negotiation in general but on a specific negotiation. It is a culture shared among the task participants. It specifies how they are to negotiate; communicate; make decisions; supervise; delegate; lead; appraise performance; manage; plan; conduct meetings; resolve conflicts; and form, maintain, and dissolve relationships. It specifies the meaning of a contract, a treaty, a policy, or an agreement in terms of time, responsibilities, comprehensiveness, and so forth. It includes at least the *minimal number* of perceptions required for getting the business done acceptably to all parties concerned.

## MCs

The parameters of an MC are determined by the **task ecology** in which the participants are doing business. That ecology includes the characteristics of the people participating in the task (their skills, objectives, and expectations based on their organizational and national culture), the task itself (its purpose, novelty, difficulty, and requirements), and the broader context in terms of facilities, resources, safety and health concerns, and time available for completion. For example, an MC is an appropriate way for us to offer technical assistance to a particular client given the motivation, knowledge, skills, resources, deadlines, and organizational and national cultures of the participants (including ourselves) involved.

Because an MC is tailored to the task ecology, *specific perceptions and ways of doing things within it are not necessarily consistent with the participants' perceptions at the organizational or national level.* This in part explains the common observation that our colleagues do not behave at all as expected given their organizational or national culture. The Japanese businessman that in many situations might reflect the "high masculinity" characteristic of Japanese culture at the national level may evidence quite a different orientation in a particular task if such is appropriate to the task ecology.

Further, *the MC associated with one occurrence of a task may be different from that associated with another occurrence of it because of changes in the task ecology.* For instance, the MC for conducting a board of directors meeting may change markedly over time as a function of changes in the company's fortunes or turnover in board members. *Different groups within the same organization may have very different MCs associated with the same tasks if the ecologies are different.* One work team may be "cohesive" and another "conflict ridden," and they may thus have very different ecological requirements for getting their business done. Those differences may not be easily recognized. This can lead to the *mis*judgment that the same ecology produces different MCs, blurring the value of understanding the **perception-ecology link.** An appreciation of this link is very important for doing business effectively at home.

Nevertheless, within an organization at home there is often sufficient ecological consistency across different occurrences of the same and different types of tasks that MCs are often quite similar to each other. In such cases, more general descriptions of how business is done at the level of organizational culture can be useful. That is commonly so within a work unit or department. But in such cases we should not lose sight of the fact that *a consistent way of doing business across tasks remains effective because the task ecology remains stable.* We should *not* forget the importance of the perception-ecology link. When doing business *between* departments or organizations or during organizational *transition*—with more variable task ecologies— descriptions at the organizational level become much less useful and those at the MC level become essential for doing business effectively.

The range of tasks potentially relevant to doing business at home is enormous. The set of *actual tasks* important to any particular business is contingent on the type of organization (commercial, governmental, educational, scientific, and so forth). Detailing the *actual tasks* likely to be encountered when doing business at home is a key part of managing that *organization.* Examples of commonly occurring tasks include negotiating, meeting, training, team building, interviewing, teaching, learning, disciplining, persuading, entertaining, participating in seminars, and decision making. Each of these, of course, could be seen as containing further "subtasks" or being subtasks themselves. Part of the challenge of detailing the actual tasks is to determine the most useful *unitization* of those tasks in terms of developing MCs. That is, should we examine MCs associated with "teaching" and "learning" separately or look at them together in an MC associated with a seminar? Should we develop an MC for negotiating a particular contract or MCs for the specific meetings that occur during that negotiation?

As with the tasks themselves, the range of perceptions potentially relevant to successful task completion is enormous. Further, because shared perceptions at the task level are rarely formalized or documented and are in any case subject to constant change, no lists of perceptions are available as with national and organizational cultures. Detailing the *actual perceptions* likely to be encountered in a specific task is key part of managing that *task*.

A given MC will consist of perceptions within a subset of the dimensions previously described at the national or organizational levels appropriate to that type of task. But an MC is manifested in the most specific and operational of ways: it is what *specific* people *actually* say and do on a *particular* occurrence of the task. Again, this may or may not be easily derivable from their organizational or national culture. Commonly, predictions derived from the latter would produce hopelessly complex, inconsistent, or confusing sets of possible perceptions for behavior at the task level. Which is the *right* one? What is the *actual* MC used to do business in that task?

In summary, the relationship between national, organizational, and microculture is depicted in Figure 3.1.

## SOME RELATED APPROACHES

Focusing on MCs as the most useful unit of analysis for studying behavior in organizations is consistent with an increasingly common theme in contemporary social science. Forgas, for instance, defines *social episodes* similarly in some respects to MCs: they are "units of social interaction, with temporal and often physical boundaries, and with a culturally known and accepted

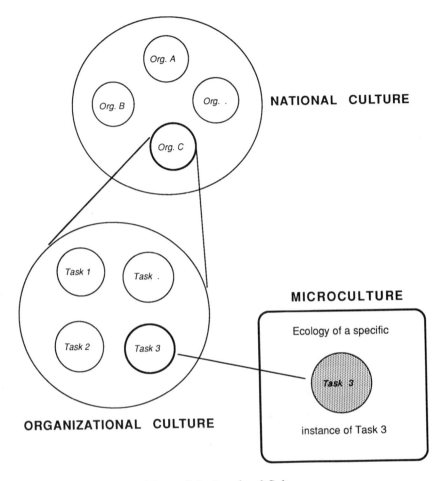

**Figure 3.1**   Levels of Culture

scheme of appropriate behaviours."[1] An MC, however, is defined *functionally* (perceptions associated with completing a task), while an episode does not necessarily imply an explicit function. Additionally, an MC is not defined so *temporally* or *spatially* as is an episode. A given MC may involve several settings, be temporally discontinuous, or even occur simultaneously with MCs associated with other tasks.

1. Forgas, J. P. (1979). *Social episodes: The study of interaction routines.* New York: Academic Press.

Further, Forgas views episodes as *abstract* descriptions of commonly reoccurring interaction sequences, not descriptions of *actual* real-life sequences. In this sense, MCs and social episodes are *fundamentally* different. An MC is "what actually happens"[2] imbedded in the ecology of a particular occurrence of a task. That is the primary thrust of the concept. However, in those cases in which the ecology remains consistent across different occurrences of a task the presumption is that MCs would be similar, abstract descriptions would then be useful, and the two approaches would be functionally equivalent.

Recent work on *practical intelligence* in business and other contexts suggests that the key to intelligent task behavior lies in tying problem-solving strategies to the environmental context in which the problem is embedded.[3-5] Practical intelligence is thinking "within a system of activity, . . . not [as] an isolated mental process . . . but an integral action directed toward some specifiable end and accomplished under specificable circumstancies."[6] In involving problem-solving strategies tailored to the task ecology, it is close to the MC concept:

> Skilled practical thinking is marked by flexibility—solving the "same problem" now one way, now another, each way *finely fitted to the occasion.* . . . Skilled practical thinking incorporates features of the task environment (people, things, information) into the problem-solving system.[7] [Emphasis added]

2. Ossorio, P. (1978). *What actually happens.* Columbia: University of South Carolina Press.

3. Klemp, G. O., & McClelland, D. C. (1986). What characterizes intelligent functioning among senior managers. In R. J. Sternberg & R. K. Wagner (Eds.), *Practical intelligence: Nature and origins of competence in the everyday world.* New York: Cambridge University Press.

4. Scribner, S. (1986). Think in action: Some characteristics of practical thought. In R. J. Sternberg & R. K. Wagner (Eds.), *Practical intelligence: Nature and origins of competence in the everyday world.* New York: Cambridge University Press.

5. Wagner, R. K., & Sternberg, R. J. (1986). Tacit knowledge and intelligence in the everyday world. In R. J. Sternberg & R. K. Wagner (Eds.), *Practical intelligence: Nature and origins of competence in the everyday world.* New York: Cambridge University Press.

6. Scribner. Thinking in action, p. 16.

7. Ibid., pp. 22–23.

Scribner and others illustrate how different strategies are tuned to different ecologies. For example, she presents results of the following research with dairy workers:

> Assemblers, classified as unskilled workers, are responsible for locating products stored in the warehouse and sending out to the loading platform the amount of each product ordered by drivers for their daily routes. Assemblers secure information about product orders from a computer-generated form that represents quantities according to a setting-specific system, using a dual metric of case and unit. Dairy products are stored and handled in standard size cases that hold a certain number of containers (units) of a given size (4 gallons, 9 half-gallons, 16 quarts, 32 pints, 48 half-pints). If a particular order involves a quantity not evenly divisible into cases, the order form represents it as a mixed number: X cases plus or minus (according to rule) 4 units. For example: 1-6 on the order form stands for one case minus 6 units. The numerical value of this expression depends on the container size it qualifies: 10 quarts, 26 pints, 4 half-pints. Whenever the assembler encounters a case-and-unit problem, he or she must interpret the symbolic representation on the form to determine the unit quantity needed, map this quantity onto the physical array, and collect as many units as will satisfy the order.
>
> In our recorded observations . . . we made the following discoveries:
>
> 1. Assemblers often departed from the literal format of the orders.
>
> 2. They filled what looked like the identical order (e.g., 1 case—6 quarts, or 10 quarts) in a variety of ways, depending on the availability of empty or partially filled cases in the vicinity. Observed solutions on this order included, for example, subtracting 4 from a partial case of 14 quarts and adding 2 quarts to a partial case of 8.
>
> 3. On all occasions, the mode of order filling, whether literal or nonliteral, was exactly that procedure that satisfied the order in the fewest moves—that is, of all alternatives, the solution the assembler selected required the transfer of a minimum number of units from one case to another . . . .
>
> 4. Mental calculations for these least-effort solutions required the assembler to switch from one base number system to another. The mental effort involved in problem transformations was increased by the fact that assemblers typically

went for a group of orders at one time, thus having to keep in mind quantities expressed in different base number systems.

5. Solutions representing least physical effort were accomplished with speed and accuracy; errors were virtually nonexistent.

6. In job simulations, only experienced assemblers consistently employed least physical effort strategies. Novice groups were literal problem solvers, filling orders only as indicated in the representations on the order form (always responding to the order "one case—6 quarts," for example, by removing 6 quarts from a full case regardless of whether more efficient alternatives were available.[8]

Scribner notes that, while "formal models of problem solving lead us to expect that repetitive problems or problems of the same logical class will be solved by the same sequence of operations (algorithms) on all occasions of their presentation," the use of formal algorithms consistently across presentations is what the *novice* or *inexperienced* do on a task.[9] Her point is analogous to that first presented in Chapter 1, and developed further in Chapter 4, that the commonly described strategies for doing business *are not* the ones used by those *sophisticated* in international business—except when those strategies fit the task ecology.

While the foregoing example involves *individual* rather than *mutual* problem solving more typical of tasks on international assignments, it does illustrate the very different approach to *real-life* tasks that differentiates the *expert* from the *novice*. As we will see, there is every reason to expect that such an approach is descriptive of those expert at doing business internationally as well as at home.

Wagner and Sternberg have found that much practical in-

---

8. S. Scribner, Thinking in action: Some characteristics of practical thought. In Robert J. Sternberg and Richard K. Wagner (Eds.), *Practical intelligence: Nature and origins of competence in the everyday world* (excerpt Assembling Products, pp. 17–18). Copyright © 1986 by Cambridge University Press.

9. Scribner. Thinking in action, p. 22.

telligence (or the strategies associated with it) may be *tacit knowledge*: knowledge that is not openly expressed and may not be explicitly provided in training, but that differentiates experts from novices.[10] They explore tacit knowledge about managing "self," "tasks," and "others" in academic and business contexts and find such knowledge very useful in discriminating between high and moderate performers. The implication for our purposes is that the importance of MCs may be part of the tacit knowledge of those doing business effectively. It may not be how they are taught or trained to do business, and it is unlikely to be the strategy to which their effectiveness is attributed by others, but it is what *actually happens!*

*The key to practical intelligence and the use of MCs is tailoring perceptions of how to do business to the task ecology* rather that simply adopting a "rule of thumb" unresponsive to that ecology. Steele has extensively examined the impact that one aspect of the ecology—the physical environment—has on doing business.[11] Focusing on what he calls *organizational ecology*, he very usefully specifies how the task environment affects perceptions of identity and ownership, social interaction, motivation, power and influence, boundary relations, organizational climate, task effectiveness, and quality of life. He is principally concerned with how to alter the ecology to support best a particular way of doing business rather than tailoring the way of doing business to a given ecology. His work reinforces the fact that we are not always at the mercy of our task ecology: *those most effective at doing business may also be those who are able to select or change ecologies to best suit their skills and resources.* I return to this issue later in the chapter.

Steele's work also contributes usefully to the topic addressed next: specifying the characteristics of specific MCs. He provides examples (see Table 3.1) of the relationship between specific characteristics of the organizational ecology and perceptions associated with doing business—perception-ecology links.

---

10. Wagner & Sternberg. Tacit knowledge.

11. Steele, F. (1980). *Making and managing high-quality workplaces: An organizational ecology.* New York: Teachers College Press.

**TABLE 3.1** Tailoring Perceptions to the Ecology*

| Perceptual Dimension | Effective Perception in Closed Layout | Effective Perception in Open Layout |
|---|---|---|
| Voice level | Lower in common areas; whatever you like in your own office | Lower in common areas and in own workplace or will be intrusive to others |
| Greeting people when you see them | Say hello when see; it's impolite not to do so | Possibly say hello first time seen that day but no more or you'll always be greeting each other |
| Entering someone's space | OK to do it unless door is closed; respect closed door as signal to stay out | OK to do it unless some signal is up saying "I'm in my private mode" (and norm should be to respect these signals) |
| Where to chat with people | Any hallway or common area is OK | Shouldn't chat right on top of someone else's workspace—forces them to be a part of the conversation even if they don't want to be |
| Talking on telephone | Talk as loudly as you like if your door is shut | Modulate your voice level so as not to blast out others around you |
| Use of radios | Personal option in own office | Group issue if others can hear it in your area |

*Reprinted by permission of the publisher from Fritz Steele, *Making money & managing high quality workplaces: An organizational ecology* (New York: Teachers College Press, © 1986 by Teachers College, Columbia University). All rights reserved.

# CHARACTERISTICS OF SPECIFIC MCS

In the same sense that we can talk about culture at national, organizational, and micro levels, so too ecological assessment can occur at each of these levels. The *task ecology* also consists of the physical, social, and biological environment with the first two generally being most significant.

- The *physical* component of the ecology commonly includes the characteristics of the specific setting(s) or facilities in which task activity occurs: urban/suburban/rural, in-doors/out-of-doors, home/car/plane/office, public/private. Other characteristics such as the distance between participants, local climate, and availability of resources are also important.
- The *social* component of the ecology commonly includes individual (competence, motivation, personality) and group (cohesiveness, conflict, familiarity, similarity) characteristics of the participants, their cultural expectations (for how to complete the task and performance standards), task objectives and structure, the relation between it and other tasks, and the time necessary to complete it.
- The *biological* component includes the degree of crowdedness, nutritional requirements, safety and security risks, and health concerns which affect the consequent need for inclusion of preventative and treatment activities in the MC.

Again, as with the range of tasks relevant to doing business and the perceptions associated with these tasks, the potential range of relevant ecological characteristics is very large. But, as we will see, the specification of the *actual* task ecology is the key to the development of an MC leading to successful completion of that task. This relationship is illustrated in the following case. The objective in presenting this case is to illustrate, using a few simple dimensions of perception and ecological characteristics, what a specific MC could be.

## Case Illustration A

An American *video production company* and an American *video distribution company* wish to negotiate a contract for the former to provide the latter with a package of new programming for release to cable networks and retail video outlets. Both companies are headquartered in Los Angeles and both agree to an afternoon meeting at the *distributor's* office. The *production company* is represented by its Marketing Manager, her Assistant, and one of their more popular writers and is bringing along "promos" of several recent productions. The *distributor* is represented by its Acquisitions Director and one of its top Promoters. Participants from both companies anticipate making at least a tentative decision on the contract by the end of the meeting.

The meeting begins with a brief social chat between the Marketing Manager and the Promoter who have had casual business contact for years. As they are chatting, the other participants introduce themselves to one another and exchange light banter about the industry. After several minutes the Acquisitions Director turns to the Marketing Manager and says, "Let's see what you've got!" From this point discussion ensues in a very informal manner with first names, frequent "industry jokes," and name dropping. Both companies initially take positions quite deviant from one another and pursue their cases with verbal aggressiveness. The general tenor of the meeting is that of a good-humored, but serious, adversarial bargaining episode with both companies pushing the strengths of their position. For the *production company* that is the quality and market appeal of their products; for the *distributor*, the risk and various alternatives for cost/risk sharing. Both companies desire to approach basic issues of programming, additional editing, cost, timing, distribution rights, and so on, separately and in sequence.

All the preceding has been rather stereotypic of negotiations the participants have been involved in previously. About midway through the meeting, with neither side giving way on anything significant, the Acquisitions Director (aware that the *production company* has had difficulty marketing products for a year and is in serious financial trouble) makes a direct comment regarding the unlikelihood that any other distributer would pick up their package. While both the Writer and Marketing Manager quickly disagree verbally, the logjam is broken, and they begin to make concessions quickly.

> By 4:30 P.M. the two companies seem to have reached
> basic agreement on all agenda items except the scope of
> distribution rights. At that point, the Marketing Manager
> privately turns to her friend the Promoter and suggests that
> all participants continue their meeting over drinks and dinner
> at a recently opened restaurant with which she is familiar.
> The Promoter relays the suggestion to the Acquisitions Direc-
> tor. The latter suggest, instead, lunch the next day in his ex-
> ecutive dining room. The Marketing Manager reluctantly
> agrees. The following day a tentative agreement is reached on
> all issues, and lunch in ended by making arrangements for
> their respective lawyers review to the deal prior signing the
> contract.

This is obviously a skeletal description. Nevertheless, shared
expectations of the participants for completion of the task form
the basis of a "bare-bones" MC. The MC draws on participant
expectations of informality, abbreviated introductory ritual, verbally aggressive bargaining, directness, and linearity in negotiation common to the American national culture. It draws on expectations of a short time frame for decision making, decision
making in the context of the meeting, and the appropriateness
of a social setting (a restaurant) for doing business common to
both their organizational cultures. It draws on perceptions of the
effectiveness of *personal* interorganizational contact (between the
Marketing Manager and Promoter) and the *direct* exercise of
power (by the Acquisitions Director) based on some specific
ecological characteristics of this particular negotiation: the friendship between two participants, the financial difficulties of the production company, and the location of the meetings.

Additionally, there appears to have been a (failed) attempt
by the Marketing Manager to change the perception of power by
moving the site of continued negotiation from the distributor's
facility to a restaurant familiar only to her. The use of ecological
cues to alter the MC is more apparent in another case presented
shortly. This first case may be quite removed from the kinds of
tasks and associated ecologies relevant to many of us. For that
reason I again suggest an exercise.

# Exercise

Stop for a moment and think about your job. What is one important task that you must complete tomorrow as part of that job?

How do you and the other participants expect to go about completing this task? That is, what perceptions are shared about how to do this task effectively? List them (you might for interest also note those perceptions that are *not* shared).

What is the ecology of that task—the physical, biological, and social environment in which it will be completed? What, for example, is the location, the temperature, the nature of the workspace, the number of employees, their skills, motivation, and personality, the resources available, the communication and information processing support, and so on? List them.

Now in what ways are the previously listed perceptions responsive to the task ecology as you've identified it? That is, do the perceptions constitute an MC tailored to the task ecology or simply reflect those at the level of national or organizational culture applicable only to this *type* of task in general? Are the perceptions more appropriate to previous tasks with somewhat different ecologies? To the degree that the perceptions *are* tailored to the ecology of your particular task, they will constitute an MC effective for doing business. That is practical intelligence. To the degree they *are not* so tailored, their effectiveness is problematic.

Think about it! Certainly an ecological assessment such as this would be valuable for a newcomer to our office or someone coming there to do business. It would indicate to them a great deal about why we perceive and do things the way we do. Perhaps some things that even *we* don't understand would become clearer.

# MANIPULATING THE TASK ECOLOGY

As noted earlier we are not always at the mercy of the ecology in how we do business. *We* do not always need to do all the accommodating. An appreciation of the perception-ecology link can allow us to influence the MC in *preferred* ways (to match our skills or ethics better, avoid our weaknesses, or change counterproductive aspects of the organizational culture) by altering key elements in the task ecology. That is the purpose behind a "retreat" for company executives, for instance: to get them out of their normal organizational ecology for a time and into one supportive perhaps of less formality, status consciousness, and conflict and more supportive of creativity and innovation. Typically this is done by altering the physical, biological, and social characteristics of the ecology—from changing the facility to changing eating, socializing, and meeting patterns. Such concerns should also be reflected in plans for building new company facilities.

We just saw how the marketing manager in Case Illustration A attempted, but failed, to alter the ecology. Case Illustration B illustrates a more successful attempt.

---

## Case Illustration B

Metpac, a medical education and training organization based in Tokyo and Honolulu, wished to develop a seminar program in which it could bring together top physicians from Tokyo with rank-and-file physicians from throughout Japan to discuss new developments in a range of medical topics. Metpac wished to develop a program of the highest academic and professional standards and at the same time allow the type of informal, interpersonal contact between different status physicians that simply does not normally occur in the status-minded Japanese national culture or medical profession. It wanted something to set its program apart from the typical medical conference in Japan.

To break the participants' expectations of formality and concerns for status purposely, the program developers decided to offer the program in Hawaii—flying both the rank-and-file and Tokyo physician/teachers out from Japan (and its ecology) for a five-day program of seminars interspersed with social and recreational activities. The physical setting was that of a relatively isolated resort hotel with centralized meeting, dining, and recreation facilities surrounded by attractively designed bungalows set amid tropical mountains and a spectacular ocean view.

The social activities were designed for the more informal, less status-conscious American culture with lots opportunities for small-group, interpersonal contact. Recreational activities were to reinforce further the informality by illustrating the relaxed life-style and "Aloha" of Hawaii. And, of course, many of the cues to Japanese medical culture would be left behind—the physical setting, hospital administrators, wives, peers, and media.

---

This case illustrates planned ecological manipulation to support development of an MC much more appropriate to the objectives of the organization than alternative strategies based on the relevant organizational or national culture. Further, adoption of this MC would be relatively unthreatening because of the necessary five-day time limit—no one would have to "suffer" the new MC too long!

## A FINAL NOTE

These last two chapters have examined how we do business at home. We have looked at the roles of perception, convergence, communication, culture, and ecology. I have emphasized the key importance of understanding MCs: we do business consistently effectively at home by developing MCs tailored to individual task ecologies. The perceptions of how to do business within these MCs are often generalized to an organizational or even national culture. However, if the ecologies are not also so generalizable, the "tailoring" is lost, and these generalized perceptions are no longer maximally effective. But commonly at home the ecology is relatively stable from task to task, and the perceptions can be extended from one to another as well. Again, organizational culture is *often* a useful concept when doing business domestically. It can specify how to complete a range of tasks effectively in this familiar ecology. But a domestic ecology *rarely* extends internationally. And it is to doing business internationally that we turn for the remainder of this book.

# DOING BUSINESS INTERNATIONALLY

# Chapter 4

When we are assigned internationally we must switch from doing business in a familiar, domestic ecology to one comprised of all those characteristics that differentiate international from domestic assignments mentioned in Chapter 1 (place, time, travel, communication, people, support, and structure), those that differentiate between international assignments (type of organization, locus of organizational identity, face-to-face versus mediated interaction, short- versus long-term assignments, a bilateral versus multilateral context, a cosmopolitan versus provincial destination, differences in technology, and a giving versus exchanging versus getting role), along with a range of task-specific characteristics. *We may or may not have the skills to do business effectively in this new ecology.*

On an international assignment, we require the skills to face two major challenges:

1. Coping with our physical, psychological, and social reaction to finding ourselves in a different ecology. That involves more than just coping with different cultures, we must cope with our reaction to *all* characteristics of the international assignment ecology that differentiate it from those we face at home or those we have faced on other assignments. We must have **the skill to cope with ecoshock** (not just culture shock!).

2. Developing a strategy to do business effectively in that ecology. This involves more than doing business in a manner compatible with another culture. We must have **the skill to do business** in a way that is compatible with *all* important characteristics of the assignment ecology.

Thus a businessman promoting his product at a summer trade fair in Guangzhou will have to cope with the stress produced by heat, humidity, language differences, and facing a very different culture. At the same time he will have to develop a strategy for using that trade fair effectively that takes these and many other characteristics of this assignment ecology into account—not the least of which is likely to be a different perspective by his hosts on the fair's objectives.

These two challenges are not, of course, independent. Failure to cope with ecoshock can exacerbate the challenge of doing business effectively: stress from the heat or language difficulties, for instance, can wear down patience at a time it is most needed to do business. On the other hand, failure to do that business effectively can exacerbate our reaction to the new ecology: frustration from not meeting expectations can add to our stress. But the challenges are not the same. The extent to which we deal with them will significantly determine the success of our assignment. We need to develop skills for *both*. To *say* that is easy; to *do* it is tough and is what this book is all about.

## COPING WITH ECOSHOCK

When we interact with people from another culture, the subsequent failure of our perceptions to be verified produces what is commonly called **culture shock:**[1,2] the world just doesn't work as it "should" any more. We smile, and they get angry. We get angry, and they ridicule us. We try to "get down to business," and they try to get away from it. We feel we've yet to accomplish anything, and they feel the task is completed. In other words, the people we are doing business with act differently from us, or differently from our stereotype of them. If lack of verification in either of these senses occurs in significant tasks (those necessary to get along personally and professionally), our reaction can be a major impediment to the success of our assignment.

While both theoretical and applied concern in international business has focused on our reaction to cultural differences, such differences are by no means the only ones we encounter on an assignment. They may or may not contribute most to our reaction to the new ecology. Differences in climate, changes in

---

1. Oberg, K. (1958). Culture shock and the problem of adjustment to new cultural environments. Washington, DC: Department of State, Foreign Service Institute.

2. Furnham, A., & Bochner, S. (1986). *Culture shock: Psychological reactions to unfamiliar environments.* New York: Methuen.

residence or living habits, new responsibilities, problems of communication with the home office, disruption of social support, or any of the other ecological characteristics presented in Chapter 1 may, on any given assignment, be more significant. Each one can produce stress.[3] In all cases, however, our reaction is to the total ecological transition—not just to any one part of it. For that reason the term **ecoshock** is more appropriate to international assignments and is defined as our reaction to ecological differences (including culture) encountered on such assignments.

In a way the term eco*shock*, like culture *shock*, is less than ideal in that "shock" connotes some acute, traumatic reaction to an identifiable event—a traffic accident, the sudden death of a loved one, the trauma of a battle—involving fainting or more serious, life-threatening reactions. There are instances when ecoshock manifests itself in this acute manner. We are literally confronted with a world seemingly "out of whack," our security appears threatened, and our reaction is the prototypical acute stress reaction. These instances are relatively rare, however. Ecoshock is usually more *chronic* than acute. It is a cumulative response to a variety of failures to predict and interact effectively in the new ecology. It is more commonly a phenomenon of weeks, months, or maybe even years than one of minutes. But it can be both!

### The Symptoms of Ecoshock

**Ecoshock is stress.**[4,5] It is stress produced by a transition in ecology, like that produced in any "transitional experience" in which people go from one ecology to another: getting married or divorced, going to college, getting a job, changing jobs, going into the military, getting out, going to prison, getting out, retir-

---

3. Holmes, T. H., & Rahe, R. H. (1967). The "Social Readjustment Rating Scale." *Journal of Psychosomatic Research, II*, 213–218.

4. Barna, L. M. (1983). The stress factor in intercultural relations. In D. Landis & R. W. Brislin (Eds.), *Handbook of intercultural training.* Vol. II: *Issues in training methodology.* New York: Pergamon.

5. Ruben, B. D. (1983). A system-theoretical view. In W. B. Gudykunst (Ed.), *Intercultural communications theory: Current perspectives.* Beverly Hills, CA: Sage.

ing, and probably just getting older.[6,7] The stress resulting from these transitions involves some reasonably predictable symptoms:

- *Poor perceptual-motor reactions* and *short-term illness* from immediate imbalance in the physiological reaction to stressors and breakdown in the resistance to disease produced by that reaction. A common occurrence on an assignment is seemingly constant illness and unusual clumsiness—both usually occurring when "least needed."

- *Long-term illness* from the wearing distress of the physiological reaction on body organs and systems. As with persons in any stressful occupation, those whose career involves lots of international assignments are at greater risk of heart, digestive, respiratory, and other serious ailments.

- *Anxiety* or nervousness, often with no specific identifiable cause. The feeling of tension for no particular reason is common. It is most often simply the product of high levels of adrenalin produced by the new ecology.

- *Depression* manifested in fatigue, wishing to sleep all the time, withdrawal from others, or the inability to get interested or excited about anything. It is seen in the spouse who stays home, closes the curtains, doesn't socialize, and sleeps all day. It is often associated with alcohol or drug abuse.

- *Irritability,* often over matters that otherwise might appear minor. Differences in traffic behavior, restaurant etiquette, or punctuality can produce exaggerated fury.

- *Fears of being taken advantage of* or cheated. This involves kind of a mild paranoia. Often there is some basis to it—we may be the target of some discrimination— but usually not to the degree perceived.

---

6. Adler, P. S. (1975). The transitional experience: An alternative view of culture shock. *Journal of Humanistic Psychology, 15*(4), 13–23.

7. Bennett, J. (1977). Transition shock: Putting culture shock in perspective. *International & Intercultural Communication Annual, 4,* 45–52.

- *Feelings of vulnerability.* Most of us, most of the time feel that we are special, somehow protected from the misfortune that affects others. We feel safe from the earthquakes, diseases, accidents, crime, terrorism, or failure we may see on the evening news. Generally we can predict events in our own familiar ecology well enough to avoid most trauma—or at least we *feel* we can. Ecoshock leaves many people, often for the first time in their lives, feeling naked and vulnerable in the world. The experience can be devastating and leads many to check for the first flight home.

- *Lowered effectiveness of cognitive processes.* The narrowing of cognitive focus produced by the physiological reaction to stressors, while certainly useful if preparing for a "fight" or "flight," often inhibits the spontaneity, creativity, flexibility, breadth of view, and analytical and integrative ability necessary for effective negotiation, problem solving, and decision making. We don't "think" as well and, again, usually at the time we need to think best.

- *Breakdown in old relationships and difficulty in establishing and maintaining new ones.* Social skills require feelings of self-assurance, naturalness, and appropriateness. These all deteriorate rapidly when we are faced with a new ecology and events we are unable to understand or predict.

These symptoms are not, of course, independent of one another: someone frequently sick is likely to feel vulnerable and depressed! And who wants to be friends with a sick, scared, depressed person?

The key to coping with ecoshock, as with other transitional experiences, is partly to understand that these symptoms are not abnormal and threatening, but are *normal* and threatening: threatening because they can interfere with getting important personal and business needs met. We *all* experience them in some pattern within a series of fairly predictable *phases* of adjustment.

### The Phases of Adjustment

Adjustment to an international assignment is typically experienced in a series of phases. We may experience all or only some of them. Going through them once does not necessarily lessen the impact of the next assignment. In practice, adjustment involves a continuous "drifting back and forth" through phases like the tide across the sand. Each phase has somewhat different implications for the degree of ecoshock experienced, the types of symptoms manifested, and the ways in which we cope. The international literature abounds with similar descriptions of such phases.[8] I have found the description presented next, adapted and expanded from Adler,[9] to be most useful.

The **contact phase** occurs at the point of initial entry into the new ecology—we just get off the plane in Singapore, or Sydney, or Paris, or New York. The phase is usually associated with excitment, positiveness, and optimism (though not always—especially if we or our spouse doesn't want to be there). We're in a new place, perhaps exotic and thrilling. It may be a place we've seen, read, or heard much about. It has a history. It may be where the "action" is. This is the phase of the "tourist." The focus is often on *similarities* between our culture and theirs, our city and theirs, our job description and theirs: isn't that cute, they shake hands, too, they have cross-walks, too, they have problems with employee discipline, too! And the focus is on *nonthreatening differences*. Differences in food are usually nonthreatening as long as we can get some of our own when we need to. In fact part of the fun of going other places is exploring different food (we do that in "ethnic restaurants" at home). Differences in clothing are nonthreatening also, unless they wear too many or too few of them. Even differences in religion are usually nonthreatening, at least at the level the architecture. Lots of our slides are of their churches, mosques, or temples!

Because we are able to maintain most of our illusions (stereotypes) about the other place, ecoshock is not very severe in the contact phase. And even if there are some early problems, many of the symptoms of ecoshock take time to develop and are not evidenced until later. People in this phase are easy to recognize. They are the excited newcomers with all the ideas, ambitious objectives, and enthusiasm. They arrive for work early and they leave late. The "old hands" will chuckle at them a bit

8. Bochner, S. (Ed.). (1981). *The mediating person: Bridges between cultures*. Cambridge, MA: Schenkman.

9. From P. S. Adler, The transitional experience: An alternative view of culture shock. *Journal of Humanistic Psychology, 15*(4), 13–23. Copyright © Sage Publications, Inc.

in a knowing way. Like the other phases, the duration of the contact phase is contingent on many factors and thus difficult to predict. Certainly two to three months is common for the person relocated overseas, though it may be much shorter for someone on an intensive, short-term assignment.

The **disintegration phase** begins with the recognition that similarities are more superficial and differences much deeper than at first perceived. We begin to see that our illusions are just that—*illusions*! The differences between ecologies are significant, and they prevent the adequate completion of the tasks necessary for working and living there. This week it may just be one thing, the next week another. Or they may all come gushing down at once! In any event, the phase is associated with confusion, frustration, and the whole range of ecoshock symptoms. It is at its first glimmerings that the tourist on the Caribbean cruise begins playing shuffleboard on deck rather than visiting the local ports—"There's always too much dirt and noise in those markets! "The businesswoman on assignment to Rio starts considering an early return— "They don't seem to *want* to do business here!"

Those in this phase are also easy to recognize. The same people who were at work early and eager last week now begin coming late, leaving early, taking sick leave, needing a break; they are inconsistent in mood, motivation, and productivity. Again, the duration is difficult to predict, but six months wouldn't be unusual. It is the time the person and his or her family begin thinking that relocation was a big mistake!

The **reintegration phase** begins as we think we understand the new ecology. We have by now been there long enough that we have, in fact, learned some things about it. We no longer feel so confused. We may be getting back to work again. But the key term here is "think." We *think* that we understand it. But most frequently the learning is far from complete. It is a phase of "re-illusion": the building of new *illusions* to replace the old ones. But because they are still illusions, they aren't effective enough in predicting the world. We continue to experience too many failures and still have high stress. We continue to manifest the symptoms of ecoshock.

Most likely because of the failures and our high stress, the stereotypes we develop are commonly negative and exaggerated: we think we understand them now, and we don't like them! "They are stupid, ignorant, lazy, crazy, rigid, loose, backward, bigoted, cheating," and so forth. The tourists that haven't left already leave now—"and I'm not going back and advise you not to go at all!" The businessperson feels similarly, and if he or she does return home at this point, future international assignments won't be relished. People in this phase are easy to recognize: they are the ones with the big mouths, derogating the host culture and environment; and they usually don't care who hears them.

Another less common reaction is overly positive stereotyping. We perceive that, once adjusted to, everything about the new place is *better* than home. We "go native." We wear the clothes, learn the dialect, and shun our home culture associates. Like converts everywhere, we become more like the host culture than the hosts. But it is an ideal, stereotyped version of the host culture, and this reaction is no more effective in the long run than the previous one.

Finally, some people alternate between negative and positive stereotypes: one day this is the best place on earth, the next day they hate it and are going home, the following day they invest in property. Their unpredictability can make interacting with them in business or social relationships difficult!

The **autonomy phase** begins as greater learning occurs, our perceptions are based more on our experiences with individuals in the host culture than on stereotypes, the world gets more predictable, we become more effective, and stress and the symptoms of ecoshock are reduced. In this phase we get on to doing business without special supports: a guide, our embassy, or a "bottle." The attitude is more like "it's business as usual" even if it's a different "usual." Ecological differences and cultural diversity are accepted, if not valued.

The objective of most cross-cultural training is to get people to the autonomy phase as quickly as possible and to keep them there for as long as possible. It's in this phase that people are most effective, but hardest to recognize because they are "normal." They are the smooth-functioning embassy staffers, engineering consultants, or visiting professors. It's important to note, however, that they will rarely remain in the autonomy phase for the duration of the assignment: events inevitably occur that will send them back, at least for a time, to reintegration, disintegration, or even contact.

### Reentry

There is another adjustment phase: that experienced on the return home. Organizations want their people to return from international assignments and continue to be productive both at home and in future assignments! **Reentry shock** is a special case of ecoshock that occurs when we return to our home ecology.[10,11] For many people, an international assignment represents one of the most significant experiences in their life—it's impact doesn't end with the arrival home! And reentry shock is no joke: it can have serious, lifelong consequences.

Those returning from assignments commonly report that reentry shock is more serious than the shock of going overseas, itself. This is in part because it is *unexpected* and *unprepared for.* Most of us anticipate difficulty in going overseas and prepare ourselves psychologically, if not through more formal training. We usually expect little difficulty in returning home. In fact, overseas we often eagerly anticipate our return, having developed a rather idealized illusion (again) of what home is like. We remember the clean supermarket, but forget the prices; we remember the ease of buying stamps, but forget the lines; we long for "seasons of the year," but forget the frustration of cars stalled by cold or roads dangerous with ice. Reentry shock is serious for a different reason as well. While we may experience ecoshock for weeks, months, or even the few years of an assignment, we will experience and must cope with reentry shock for the rest of our lives!

If we have been away on assignment for very long—a month, a year, two years—our home has changed. We often forget that as many things have happened at home *without* us as have happened overseas *to* us. Home has changed, and we can never really catch up. Tracking events from afar (through newspapers, magazines, letters, and company reports) is not the same as participating in them. Most of us don't realize that keeping up with

---

10. Martin, J. (1984). The intercultural reentry: Conceptualization and directions for future research. *International Journal of Intercultural Relations, 8,* 115–134.

11. Sussman, N. M. (1986). Re-entry research and training: Methods and implications. *International Journal of Intercultural Relations, 10,* 235–254.

our culture while living *in* it is a full-time job. Any time spent away is a gap. If the gap is large, we and those we relate to will always feel it: if only as awkwardness in the simple interactions that before had flowed so naturally. When our friends finish listening to a story or two from our travels and they begin to talk of "whatever" happened in the office during the week, we don't know what to say! Remember that people *diverge* from those with whom they are not interacting: for our family and business associates back home, that's us!

If we were filling any important roles in our organization, family, or social network and if we have been gone for any significant period of time, upon our return those roles will be filled by others. Important roles simply cannot go vacant for very long. So we arrive home without a place: the student coming home to find her bedroom allocated to a younger sibling, the employee coming home to find the same of office, secretary, and responsibilities. And it can truly be a shock! We feel like a visitor again, and we thought we were finished with that. We're not prepared to repeat the experience so soon, at home!

Further, in experiencing the phases of adjustment just described, *we have changed*! We are different. And, if we weren't aware of it on the assignment, we quickly become aware of it on our return. Our family and associates at home may seem provincial, or prejudiced, or naive, or rigid, or just boring. We feel alienated. And to them *we* are like a "foreigner." We give them some culture shock—and they're not getting paid for it! They may tolerate a few hours of our slides, new clothes, or strange ideas, but we must get ourselves back together (become who we were) quickly, or they won't know what to do with us. They won't know what responsibilities to assign us. They begin avoiding us. The boss may suggest another assignment: "You seem better suited for that (and we don't know quite how to use you here)."

Further still, on international assignments we are often treated very well by our hosts. We socialize with those at the highest levels in fancy hotels, clubs, and restaurants. We stand out, *feel special*. We are part of the "international scene." There is excitment and adventure. We're on a "high." *It's hard to come down.* Back home we are lost in the crowd, at the office, at home. That's a shock. Many yearn for the "high" again for the rest of their lives. They talk about their time overseas like ex-athletes or veterans talk of old games or wars. It was the time in their lives they were most alive. They pull out their "trophies" (slides, souvenirs) to bring that time back. Or they return overseas. The student returns to where she studied, the Peace Corps worker becomes an international refugee worker, the businessman begins a career-long series of international assignments. But, of course, they are not "home" there either, and a life-style of bouncing from one place to another looking alternatively for a "home" or a "high" begins. It's the life of the lifelong expatriate.

So coping with ecoshock is one of the two primary challenges that face us on an international assignment. It is necessary for us to understand the normalcy of experiencing its phases. Beyond this understanding, coping with it principally involves good preparation and the management of stress. We turn to these later, but first we must examine carefully the other and, I propose, more important challenge.

## DOING BUSINESS EFFECTIVELY

We turn now, and in the next chapter, to the orientations people have to doing international business and the specific strategies they develop within each to do it effectively.

### Commonly Described Orientations

There are a number of commonly described orientations to doing international business, and each implies a strategy for doing that business most effectively. Each emphasizes the "cultural difference" characteristic of the assignment ecology: that is, they do business differently from how we do business so how do we all do it together? These orientations and their associated strategies are presented in the paragraphs that follow. In the real world, of course, we may go from one orientation to another frequently over the course of a career, or an assignment!

**People everywhere are the same.** In this orientation *cultural* diversity is simply not recognized. We may be aware that those confronted in other countries act differently, but we tend to attribute those differences to *individual* aberrations in perceptions or behavior: the same individual differences we encounter at home. We don't attribute the differences to culture, although we might conclude that there are more people "crazy" or "lazy" over there than at home! Those with this orientation are sometimes called "parochial,"[12] but they are not always so unsophisticated: people *are* the same and they *are* different. The issue is, in the context in which we are doing business, are the differences or the similarities more important?

The *strategy* for doing business internationally for us with this "people are the same" orientation is to try to do it the same way we do at home: that is, to do it *Our Way* as illustrated in the following case.

---

### Case Illustration C

In attempting to sell his company's new model of vacuum cleaner to retailers in the West Indies, a British sales representative scheduled meetings in Martinique, Barbados, St. Lucia, St. Vincent, and Grenada in successive days. This schedule would allow him to complete his business and return home in one efficient week. He intended on each stop to meet the retailers, demonstrate his product, and either take orders at that point or have them forwarded to his home office in London. This is how he did it at home and how his company wanted it done. The product would "sell itself." This was his *Our Way*.

---

**People elsewhere are different but our way is best.** In this orientation cultural differences are recognized, but are judged from our own perspective alone. We commonly see other ways of doing things as inadequate or a source of problems: "You have an interesting culture, but now that we must get down to business we better do it my way." This is sometimes called an "ethnocentric"[13] or "cultural dominance"[14] orientation.

---

12. Adler, N. (1986). *International dimensions of organizational behavior.* Boston: Kent.

13. Ibid.

14. Dinges, N. G., & Maynard, W. S. (1983). Intercultural aspects of organizational effectiveness. In D. Landis & R. W. Brislin (Eds.), *Handbook of intercultural training.* Vol. II: *Issues in training methodology.* New York: Pergamon.

The strategy for doing business internationally for us with this "our way is best" orientation is again to try to do it *Our Way*: not this time from failure to recognize diversity, but from *nonacceptance*[15] of the other culture's way as illustrated in the next case.

---

### Case Illustration D

The general manager of a Canadian-Malaysian joint shipbuilding venture in Malaysia was concerned over slumping productivity due to poor worker morale. He attributed the morale problems to the authoritarian style of the supervisors (mostly ethnic Chinese and Indians): in most task situations they simply *told* the workers (mostly ethnic Malays) how to complete the task properly. The general manager felt that a participatory style in which the workers were brought into the planning process would be more effective. He recognized that this style would be unfamiliar to his supervisors and workers, but he had seen such participation work for the company back home in situations involving morale difficulties. Further, he wanted his supervisors to "understand" the problem better so they would see the necessity for change and feel as though *they* were participating in it. Thus he wanted to implement his *Our Way* at two levels. His strategy was to bring in a consultant to help his supervisors both learn and implement the new style.

---

**People elsewhere are different so we must do it their way.** In this "when in Rome do as the Romans" orientation, cultural differences and the practical necessity of accepting them are recognized. We do not necessarily think their way of doing business is best, but we do see futility in trying to impose our own way.

The *strategy* for doing business internationally for us with this orientation is to try to do it *Their Way*: the ideal business-person is someone who is able to blend, to go from culture to

---

15. Seelye, H., & Wasilewski, J. (1979). Toward a taxonomy of coping strategies used in multicultural settings. Unpublished paper presented at the Society for Intercultural Education, Training and Research, Mexico City.

culture skillfully adopting the perceptions and behaviors of the culture in which he or she is doing business at the time. The orientation can also be manifested in the belief that *"somebody* must do it *Their Way."* In this latter case the strategy is to contract with host country "third parties," agencies, or "local managers" and the *international* assignment then becomes setting up the contract with them.

---

### Case Illustration E

A French cosmetic company attempted to market a product in Japan using a Japanese type of "mood-based" television advertisement which appealed to the well-documented Japanese concern for tradition. A lovely woman was seen strolling through a garden near an apparently ancient temple with only the slightest whisper of the product name in the sound of the breeze. Similar advertisements were planned for print media. The company's strategy in this case was to do business *Their Way.*

---

**People elsewhere are different so we must compromise.** In this orientation, cultural differences and the need to accept at least *some* of them are recognized: we don't want to "give in" and accept their way completely, and we are realistic enough not to expect them to do so either. We see the necessity of negotiating some combination of *Their Way* and *Our Way.* The ratio between them is influenced by the power relationship between the participants stemming from the "giving" versus "exchanging" versus "getting" character of the ecology.

The *strategy* for doing business internationally for us with this orientation is, then, to try to *Compromise*: to sometimes do it *Our Way* and sometimes *Their Way,* or combine elements of both in a "synthesis."[16,17] Typically we try to make *Compromise* easier by finding as many similarities as possible and thus limiting the number of issues that must be negotiated.

---

16. Ibid.
17. Bochner. *The mediating person.*

---

## Case Illustration F

Recently the U.S. government brought charges against alleged high-ranking members of Japan's largest underworld—or "Yakuza"—organization for gun and drug smuggling. It contended that the Yakuza members came to the United States to exchange drugs for guns with undercover agents. They presented evidence, including a secretly videotaped meeting, which they claimed would prove that the defendants verbally agreed to a smuggling deal set up by the agents.

The defense, on the other hand, asserted that the defendants were in the United States to follow up on the whereabouts of money paid to set up a rock concert in Japan. The defense contended that the agents showed them displays of weapons that could be made available to them and assured them that arrangements could be made both to get the drugs into the United States and the guns into Japan without problems. The defense asserted that the agents catered to the defendants by entertaining them lavishly in the "Asian style." That is, the agents attempted to do business somewhat *Their Way* to gain their trust. And then when the defendants said *hai* (roughly "yes" in Japanese) in response to a direct question as to whether they wished to conclude a deal they were arrested—the agents' *Our Way*. While guns and drugs are not the usual stuff of international study, they are unquestionably international business. And in this case the government used a *Compromise* strategy.

---

Any of the commonly described strategies just presented *can* be effective on a given occasion. None of them, however, are "rules of thumb" that will work on all occasions. In fact, all the cases illustrated ended in failure. And they failed for the same general reason: the strategy was not appropriate to the ecology of the particular tasks confronted on the assignment.

In Case Illustration C the sales representative didn't take any vacuum cleaner orders back with him from the West Indies nor did his home office subsequently receive any. The "efficient" trip failed because the representative didn't take into account the irregularity of air flights in that region (*he* missed a couple of meetings), the irregularity of West Indian concern for punctuality (*they* missed a couple of meetings), and the necessity to take time to establish a relationship with clients (the meetings that were held were brief and *product* oriented, not *relationship* oriented).

In Case Illustration D, following training in and an attempt to implement a participatory style, productivity continued to decline. The attempt to make supervisors more participatory largely failed because they had experienced a rapid succession of general managers and were not motivated to learn the approach of another. Their less than enthusiastic attempts to improve worker morale through participation failed because ethnic conflicts made such participation difficult. In fact there was evidence that participation allowed for *increased* ethnic conflict in some work groups. Further, worker morale was low, principally because there had been a major layoff and there were unsubstantiated rumors of another. The problem here was more *communication* than *supervision*. What was needed was a strategy more tailored to the actual ecology faced in this joint venture. For instance, a middle management team representing all ethnicities could have been much better informed as to the general manager's plans. With more information and supervisor/worker trust, they would be in a better position to stop the rumors and the downward spiral in morale.

In Case Illustration E, the *Their Way* advertisement also failed and the strategy was changed. Tradition *is* important in Japan, and it is often necessary to consider in many business contexts including advertising. But people, including the Japanese, change. Many young Japanese are attracted by foreign products (particularly European) and like to feel trendy. They weren't motivated to buy by the appeal to tradition.

In Case Illustration F, the *Compromise* strategy failed as well. The government ignored cultural differences in the role of "meetings" in the decision-making process: Americans commonly see decisions as the reason for a meeting and expect to make them during it; Japanese are more likely to use a meeting to "get-to-know" their counterparts prior to making decisions elsewhere. The government ignored the Japanese concern with "face" and the tendency to be polite and cooperative: more than Americans, Japanese are reticent to openly express disagreement— particularly to their hosts. And they ignored differences in the meaning of "yes": to Americans it usually means an affirmative; to the Japanese the meaning is more like "yes, but . . ."; or it may simply indicate that the speaker follows what is being said. The apparent assumption by the agents was that the Yakuza were agreeing to the deal. However, one could reasonably infer that the defendants were uncomfortable with the pressure and were simply trying to get through the meeting without offending the agents to discuss later the merits of the offer. The government additionally neglected a very salient characteristic of the *trial* ecology: the case was tried before a jury in Hawaii where appreciation of these cultural differences is high (about 25 percent of the population is of Japanese descent). The verdict was *not guilty*.

### What Must Actually Happen

For people with any of the orientations just presented the major preparation for doing business effectively on international assignments has been to *train* for it. For those with "people everywhere are the same" and "our way is best" orientations, the emphasis has been primarily on *technical* and *language* training. With the increasing popularity of the "we must do it their way" and "we must compromise" orientations, the last two decades have seen the rapid expansion of *cross-cultural* training programs. Most commonly these latter programs teach us how to understand other cultures better and how they do business. The basic premise has been "If we're going to do business with the Chinese (or Japanese, or French, or Americans, or whomever), we must learn how they do it" so we can do it *Their Way* or *Compromise*.

But the way people do business with one another in their own culture is not necessarily how they would do it with us. As we saw in the last chapter, those consistently effective in doing business at home do so by tailoring their ways of doing it to the task ecologies they face. We, and everything we bring with us on the assignment, are *not* part of that domestic task ecology. If they are good, they will recognize that fact and adjust their ways of doing business accordingly. Thus, cross-cultural training tells us what someone from another culture is *used to* thinking and doing—and perhaps what he or she is *good at*—but not necessarily what he or she *expects* or will *think* or *do* in interaction with us!

When we do business with internationally sophisticated Indonesians (for instance), they won't expect us to do it *Their Way*. With rare exceptions we never could. It has taken a *career* for *them* to learn how to do it effectively that way. *We are not going to learn through training in one week or one year.* To attempt to do business *Their Way* will be viewed by them as humorous or insulting or evidence of our own naivité and lack of international sophistication. It's patronizing on our part—how could we expect to do well so quickly on something they've spent all their lives learning unless we feel superior? And they feel at least our equal. The "old hands" in our office will view our attempts similarly, often with a knowing chuckle!

---

### Case Illustration G

A colleague vividly recalls trying to keep up with a bank president and his entourage in Kuala Lumpur in an attempt to secure a favorable loan for a joint venture. Dinner led to "routine" all-night drinking and entertainment among those involved in negotiating several business deals. He ended up making rather of fool of himself with several of the accompanying exquisitely presented female "singers" after consuming large quantities of alcohol. He had even been warned ahead of time by a third party that this setting might not be the best for *him* to do business. But he had tried to do it *Their Way*. No loan ever eventuated.

---

We cannot, in fact, learn how the other culture does business well enough to do it *Their Way*. And for the same reason they cannot learn ours well enough to do it *Our Way*. Nor can we commonly learn each others' sufficiently to *Compromise*. If we had to rely on these strategies international business would rarely get done well. Thus, *there must be other strategies*, and most cross-cultural training misses the point. Further, on an international assignment we do not do business with a "nation" or even an "organization." *We do business with specific people on specific tasks.* So information provided in training on how people in a nation or an organization typically do business may not be appropriate to the specific people and tasks with which we will be engaged. Finally, all the orientations presented here focus on the cultural difference characteristic of the international assignment ecology. While that characteristic is certainly important, it is by no means the only one to which we must tailor our strategy for doing business.

Thus, I propose that the commonly described strategies for doing business internationally simply do not reflect *what must actually happen* for that business to be done consistently effectively. Emphasis is on "consistent" because it is assumed that most of us sent on assignments will meet with *occasional* successes. Such successes, however, can be produced by situation-specific or fortuitous reasons: being in the right place at the right time, being lucky. Identification of strategies leading to *consistent* success has more useful implications for the management of *all* our assignments.

Previous work by myself and colleagues and extensive review of salient research leads me to propose that the optimal strategy for doing business consistently effectively on international assignments involves developing MCs appropriate to the ecology of the tasks that must be completed on each assignment. I label them **international microcultures** (or simply **IMCs**) to emphasize that they are cultures developed at the task level to do business internationally. Other terms have been used to describe related concepts ("third cultures," "diplomatic cultures," or "international cultures"), but none of these refer directly to what is intended here. An IMC is not simply *people* who are engaged in international business: it is a *way of doing business*. IMCs are what we must develop to meet the challenge of doing business effectively in international ecologies.

*That is the FIRST THEME of this book.*

---

### Case Illustration H

Earlier in my own career I was faced with providing "in-house" communication seminars to middle management personnel in a traditional, Chinese "family-owned" company in Hong Kong. My typical strategy in presenting such seminars—my *Our Way*—was to use a very interactive, participative style in which much of the communication behavior examined is elicited from seminar participants during the session. But I had had some less than optimally successful previous experience with that way in Hong Kong. From that experience I knew that the participants in this seminar would be more familiar with a more formal, lecture format and would probably be uncomfortable with an interactive one (particularly in English rather than Cantonese). The temptation, then, was to do it *Their Way*.

From my experience, however, I also knew that a few other ecological characteristics had to be considered. First, I was not particularly good at doing it *Their Way*: I was too young to receive the *ascribed* status needed to give a lecture with legitimacy in Chinese culture. I needed to achieve that legitimacy by *demonstrating* my competence to them. Second, I knew that often Chinese management personnel—aware of the recent emphasis on "participation" but unexposed to it within their company—are very anxious to try it out away from the office in a different ecology such as that presented by a western trainer in a hotel meeting room. Finally, the latter motivation not withstanding, I expected that many of them would be reticent to try it out using English in front of the other participants.

So the strategy I selected was one more tailored to the *actual* ecology confronted in that particular seminar. I integrated lectures on key issues in English with participatory small-group sessions in which the language used was often Cantonese. I was able to place a few participants found to have North American educational backgrounds in different work groups as facilitators. I demonstrated my competence by illustrating issues that participants had actually experienced in these groups. They had the opportunity to try out a more participatory style in their own language and in nonthreatening small groups. The strategy was to develop an IMC. The outcome was a successful seminar for all involved.

It should be clear that developing the IMCs referred to in the first theme and illustrated in this case is a *generic strategy*: a strategy for selecting specific strategies that are most likely to be effective in a given task. Occasionally the specific strategy chosen might be *Our Way* or *Their Way* or a *Compromise*. That would occur if one of them were most appropriate to the task ecology. In such cases, use of an IMC strategy would appear indistinguishable from it. But in those cases the specific strategy would not be effective because it is *the* way to do business internationally, but simply because it happens to be appropriate to a particular task ecology. This is shown in the next case. The strategy would rarely be effective across a range of tasks and assignments because international assignment ecologies usually differ markedly from the domestic ecology to which it is appropriate: we must, again, not lose sight of the perception-ecology link!

---

## Case Illustration I

Royal Nepal Airlines Corporation (RNAC) developed a cooperative agreement with an airline from a European country in which the latter would provide technical, marketing, operations, and publicity assistance. A project chief was assigned to RNAC who coordinated three other compatriots as advisors to three RNAC departments. The general strategy of the European airline was to help RNAC do it *Our Way*. In spite of initial optimism by both parties, however, the agreement was eventually terminated. With one exception there had been no significant improvement in the performance of any unit. That exception was the Training Section of the Maintenance Department. Their advisor was responsible for implementing a structure based on that of his own airline and specified in a detailed manual. In that lone unit, however, the *Our Way* strategy worked. In terms of the preceding discussion, it is revealing to see why.

Most units in RNAC were largely staffed by long-time company personnel who were resistant to outside input. Their resistance was further hardened by what they saw as an arrogant "tone" to the way the input was provided—the advisors apparently treated the Nepalese personnel more like inexperienced "students" than "professionals" seeking assistance. The Training Section, uniquely, was staffed by newly hired engineers who had recently completed their university educations. They had yet to develop a unit "culture," were anxious for a structure that would provide them with some explicit program direction, and wanted to see themselves in a meaningful role in the company that would facilitate career growth. The very detailed manual for their unit provided by their advisor, defining an ambitious role for training, was just what they were looking for. They adopted it energetically, overlooking that "tone" with which it was provided.

In this case *Our Way* worked, but *not* because it was *the* effective strategy for delivering assistance within the cooperative agreement (in all but the Training Section it failed!). It worked because in this one unit it was responsive—apparently fortuitously—to the ecology.[18]

Many of the initial "clues" to the first theme came from participants in training seminars conducted in several countries. When *critical incidents* of their international problems were elicited, they rarely specified problems at the organizational or national levels. They described problems principally at the task level: that is, they said "Mr. Beta is a hassle to negotiate with" much more frequently than "Company Alpha has not been a desirable partner" or "I can't work with Americans." Further, they commonly noted that their expectations for their foreign counterparts' behavior based on national stereotypes were constantly being violated: those counterparts sometimes behaved as expected, but more often did not. Behavior, in other words, seemed to depend on the task at hand much more than on culture at some more abstract level. Further, from descriptions of their attempts to deal with problems and the outcome of those attempts, it became clear that those who appeared more effective used strategies tailored to task ecologies. Sometimes the tailoring appeared to be conscious; more commonly it seemed the product of an intuitive feel for what would work best.

Subsequent examination of recent research in problem solving, negotiation, communication, intercultural relations, and management reinforced these impressions and provided the beginnings of a model of the IMC strategy. In the next chapter this model is examined more fully. By way of summary, this and the more commonly described strategies for doing business internationally are included in Figure 4.1.

## A FINAL NOTE

By proposing that IMCs are the optimal basis of consistent effectiveness, I *am not* saying that those effective on international

---

18. Bhawuk, D. P. S. (1988). Incharge, Technical Facility, RNAC. Personal Communication.

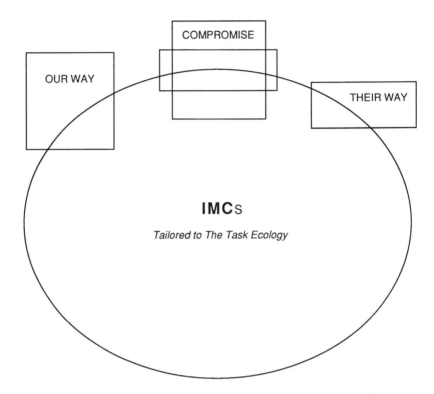

**Figure 4.1**   Strategies for Doing Business Internationally

assignments never do some things *Our Way* or *Their Way* or *Compromise*. There are lots of good reasons for doing some things *Their Way*, for instance. Among them are showing respect and good intentions, helping build relationships, and participating in the "ritual" exchanges necessary to indicate membership in the international community. It is often important that we do such things for such reasons. But I *am* saying that they are rarely the primary basis of our success.

# INTERNATIONAL MICROCULTURES

Chapter 5

An *IMC* consists of a set of perceptions about how to do business in a specific task on an international assignment. It is a culture *shared* among the participants in that task. In using IMCs internationally we are doing nothing really different from what we are when using MCs at home: we are doing business in a manner tailored to the task ecologies we face. If we are responsive to the international characteristics of those ecologies, then we are using IMCs. If we are not, we are simply imposing, accepting, or compromising on some other perceptions of problematic relevance and effectiveness.

## IMCs

An IMC is usually *not* some mixture of "our" perceptions or "their" perceptions of how to do business on a particular task. Such combinations are descriptive of a compromise strategy. They would only comprise an IMC strategy if they were ecologically appropriate. As noted in the last chapter, this would rarely be the case.

Further, an IMC like any microculture is associated with a particular occurrence of a task and will differ from that associated with other occurrences as the task ecology differs. An IMC, in other words, is *not* a generalized way to do business across many occurrences of a task. For example, the IMC used to negotiate a particular "fishing rights" treaty will nearly always differ from that used with other "fishing rights" treaties negotiated at other times and, perhaps, other participants. Because an IMC is tailored to a particular task ecology, participant perceptions about doing business within it are not necessarily consistent with their perceptions across this and other types of tasks at the organizational or national level. This explains the common observation that our foreign counterparts do not behave as expected given their organizational or national culture. This is why appreciation of the task ecology of international assignments is so critical. That ecology may differ significantly from the national or organizational ecologies and associated cultures to which our expectations of their behavior are tied.

The range of tasks potentially relevant to an international assignment is at least as large as that applicable domestically. An IMC specifies how participants in international business are to negotiate; communicate; make decisions; supervise; delegate; lead; appraise performance; manage; plan; conduct meetings; resolve conflicts; form, maintain, and dissolve relationships; train; build teams; interview; teach; learn; discipline; persuade; entertain; participate in seminars; and so forth. The set of *actual* tasks that are important on any particular assignment is contingent on the type of international business context, for example, commerce, diplomacy, advising, or foreign study. Detailing those tasks is a key part of the management of that assignment.

As with the tasks themselves, the range of perceptions potentially relevant to a particular task internationally is at least as large as that applicable to a similar task domestically. An IMC specifies at least the minimal number of perceptions required for doing business acceptably to all parties concerned. It is kind of a "bare-bones" culture. Much more than culture at the organizational or national levels, it is limited to what is *functionally necessary*. It generally doesn't involve "aesthetics"; it is most often too short-lived for the development of ritual; it has little impact beyond the parameters of the task. In negotiating the "fishing rights" treaty, we do *not* need to come to agreements on how to raise children, what constitutes good art, or what is the best system of financial accounting. We *do* need to agree on how far national sovereignty extends into the seas, appropriate surveillance, and enforcement. Detailing the *actual* perceptions likely to be useful in that task is another key part of the management of that assignment and is determined by the task ecology.

The task ecology includes the ecological characteristics that set international assignments apart from domestic assignments and apart from one another and those specific to the task (see Chapter 1). The relevance of several of these to IMCs is illustrated shortly. First, however, it should be stressed that a typical characteristic of the ecology is that participants differ in organizational and national cultures. That is, part of the ecology with which an IMC must deal are the differences in how participants habitually do business and the consequent skills they bring with them. Thus any IMC must be one compatible with what all participants *can do*, but not necessarily what they are *used to doing*, are *trained to do* in this type of task, or *think is best*. We may, for instance, be trained to arrive at pricing agreements in a contract through bargaining, but such a tactic may be inconsistent skills of our hosts. If so, it is better—if we have the skill (and we should)—to determine beforehand the best offer we can make and go with it. Otherwise our continual revision of prices during bargaining may lower our hosts' perception of both our expertness and trustworthiness and sabotage the deal.

Within IMCs new rules may emerge for doing business. While we never become truly independent of our own culture, assignments in which IMCs are created may be one of the few instances in which *individual differences* (that is, *un*shared perceptions) are better predictors of behavior than culture. On an assignment to Mexico City, we can explore ways of doing business relatively unconstrained by our own culture's norms and expectations. In some instances these new ways may fit better the skills and resources we possess than the ways preferred by our culture. In the words of Murray, "we become who we are."[1] As such there may be more behavioral variability on international assignments. This freedom to step outside the expectations of others and the norms they produce, this freedom to "become who we are" (or at least explore other ways to be) may be one of the great appeals of the international life-style—and one of the biggest adjustments to make when returning home!

An IMC has a subjective or psychological manifestation in that (as with any culture) it exists most significantly as shared perceptions in the minds of the participants. This manifestation is the principal focus here. But (also as any culture) it has a social manifestation in the people, themselves: their identity, their personality, their relationships, and the settings in which they interact. **IMC networks** are people who commonly use this strategy when doing international business: both visitors and hosts. They represent the key support group for international assignments

1. Murray, G. (1977). The inner side of cross-cultural interaction. In D. Batchelder & E. G. Warner (Eds.), *Beyond experience*. Society for Intercultural Education, Training and Research.

(see Chapter 10). As Desatnick and Bennett stress, the person doing international business must develop "a cadre of globally-minded executives, upon whom he can rely as joint custodians of the welfare of his business, both in the short and long term."[2]

## SOME RELATED APPROACHES

In their classic study of Americans overseas Useem, Useem, and Donoghue describe binational **third cultures** in a manner related to IMCs, though more in the *social* sense just briefly described.[3] They note that these third cultures are "remarkably" similar from one host country to another and that they are learned and passed on from generation to generation. Gudykunst, Wiseman, and Hammer, focusing on *satisfaction* with living and working in another culture, identify a **third culture perspective** seen as facilitating that satisfaction.[4] Neither approach, however, conceptualizes culture at the task level or emphasizes its relationship to the task ecology.

Zartman and Berman's discussion of the necessity of developing a **formula** for international diplomatic negotiation is closer to the IMC strategy presented here. A formula is:

> best characterized as a shared perception or definition of the conflict that establishes terms of trade, the cognitive structure of reference for a solution, or an applicable criterion of justice. . . . When they look for a formula . . . the parties try to find a definition of the situation that will meet the requirements of both sides and at the same time will permit a solution.[5]

---

2. Desatnick, R. L., & Bennett, M. L. (1977). *Human resource management in the multinational company*. New York: Nichols, p. 310.

3. Useem, J., Useem, R., & Donoghue, J. (1963). Men in the middle of the third culture: The roles of American and non-western people in cross-cultural administration. *Human Organization*, Fall, 169–179.

4. Gudykunst, W. B., Wiseman, R. L., & Hammer, M. (1977). Determinants of the sojourner's attitudinal satisfaction: A path model. In B. Rubin (Ed.), *Communication Yearbook I*. New Brunswick, NJ: Transaction Books.

5. Zartman, I. W., & Berman, M. R. (1982). *The practical negotiator*. New Haven, CT: Yale University Press, pp. 95–96.

Admitting that the perspective is "bold," they stress that "a search for a broad framework that will justify detailed agreements is both the way the best negotiators do proceed and the way negotiators in general should proceed."[6]

Even closer to the IMC strategy is that suggested by Kindel for negotiations between Americans and Chinese. He describes his model as:

> the required mental orientation which allows for the application of cultural learning to the negotiation process . . . . The model suggests that understanding the Chinese cultural values is the starting point for training of our management team. . . . The next step is the most difficult as it is the application of this cultural learning to the business setting. At some point, to be effective our management team must have a "feeling" for the cultural values as application in the real world requires a flexibility beyond the memorization of values. . . . With an idea of how our trading partner thinks, we can have a higher probability of developing successful . . . strategies for the negotiating table.[7]

The key to his model, then, is not to do it *their way* but to take it into consideration, have a "feeling" for it, and develop a strategy responsive to it. He illustrates how knowledge of Chinese values leads to expectations of their behavior which can lead to useful response strategies. He gives the example that understanding the Chinese value placed on "love of hierarchy and status divisions" could lead to:

### Expected Behaviors[7]

1. There will be a strong preference to negotiate with top executives of the Western firm.
2. Formal titles will be used in addressing others face to face when in public.
3. The structure will be very bureaucratic, with many levels of superiors with whom they must check.

---

6. Ibid., p. 133.

7. From T. I. Kindel, Negotiations between East and West: A cultural format. Unpublished manuscript. The Citadel, Charleston, SC.

4. No questioning of the opinion of superiors will be tolerated.
5. Each person's position of authority will be very clear at all times.
6. The other party will be expected to follow up on suggestions made through the use of formal channels of communication.

### Strategic Responses[8]

1. One should upgrade the title of executives involved in China trade.
2. The firm should send its top officers, if possible, rather than only the "manager of Asian affairs."
3. Use of formal channels of communication is necessary rather than circumventing them.
4. Proposals must be presented with conviction but there must be some flexibility built in for the specific terms.

The advantage of his model is that it specifies a clear response strategy that isn't necessarily *their way* but is responsive to it. He deals with culture largely at the national level, but conceptualizes its impact in terms of "expectations" that allow for variation at the micro level. His model, however, does not deal with the role of other characteristics likely to impact the task ecology.

As we saw in Chapter 3, recent work on practical intelligence suggests that the key to intelligent task behavior lies in tying problem-solving strategies to the environmental context in which the problem is embedded. This concept is thus closely related to both the MC and IMC concepts. The implication is that the usefulness of IMC development may be part of the tacit knowledge that differentiates those consistently effective on international assignments from those less so.

## CHARACTERISTICS OF SPECIFIC IMCs

The perceptions and ways of doing business within IMCs can vary considerably from one to another. The amount of variability is

---

8. Ibid., pp. 10–13.

limited only by parameters of usefulness defined by the task ecology.

## The Task Ecology

A specific IMC is in part based on the ecological similarities between international assignments that set them apart from domestic assignments: place, time, travel, communication, people, support, and structure. They, again, are what allows us to talk about "international assignments" in the first place. For example, IMCs must involve a way of doing business that addresses the ecological fact that visitors are typically far from home, have to travel to get there, have tight deadlines, have difficulties in communicating with the home office and obtaining adequate support, and may differ in culture and language from their hosts. The necessity of dealing with these characteristics provides a degree of consistency between different IMCs and sets them apart from domestic MCs. An attempt to do international business in a way that does not take them into account is unlikely to be *consistently* effective.

Hofstede suggests that since there are **ecological universals** associated with the circumstances for living such as the helplessness of infants, the need for food, warmth, and sex and the presence of people of different sexes, ages, and capabilities there may be **cultural universals**: if not in the way these circumstances are dealt with, then at least in that they are all dealt with.[9] In a similar manner IMCs may have much in common with each other because of the common ecological characteristics of international assignments: all IMCs may not deal with each characteristic the same way, but they must all deal with each.

An example of the impact of ecological similarities might be something like the following. Both the effects of jet lag associated with travel and the strain on attention associated with communicating in a nonprimary language suggest that a perceived way of doing business appropriate to many IMCs would involve *shorter meetings* with *frequent breaks*. The nonprimary language and lack of a history of doing business together would

---

9. Hofstede, G. (1984). *Culture's consequences: International differences in work-related values.* Beverly Hills, CA: Sage.

suggest the necessity for *more elaborated communication* and *less reading-in of hidden meanings*. That same lack of history and the concomitant opportunity to develop trust—so important in some cultures—suggests the usefulness of *more complete documentation* of organizational philosophy, the *participation of higher-status personnel*, and *greater opportunity for socializing* and *perspective sharing* than might otherwise be the case. And these might replace reliance on ritual sharing to achieve trust since ritual is so culture specific. The need for the visiting participants to remain in excellent communication with their home office and their need to replace lost organizational and social support suggests *greater appropriateness of an international class hotel* as a meetingplace than might be the case domestically. And given cultural differences and the relative improbability of future contact if the business does not go well, a good reminder in an IMC might be "when in doubt, don't get offended!"

On the other hand, ecological differences between assignments will set one IMC apart from another: type of organization, locus of identity, face-to-face versus mediated interaction, short- versus long-term assignments, and so forth. Additionally, an IMC will be based on a range of task-specific characteristics: task objectives from different participants' point of view, the facility in which the task takes place, the number of participants, their relationships, their capabilities, their motives for being there, and—importantly—their expectations for the task based on the national and organizational cultures they bring with them. These ecological differences are what makes it difficult to describe a general IMC. But based on both ecological similarities and differences, we can begin to specify ways of doing business that can be usefully included in a specific IMC. Let's return to the American Video Production Company from Case Illustration A presented in Chapter 3.

---

## Case Illustration J

The American *video production company* sends the same team to Tokyo to negotiate a contract with a Japanese *distribution company* for its package of new programming. On this assignment the American team could approach the task: (1) *Our Way* (use the aggressive, verbal, informal, short-time-frame, bargaining MC they used with the other distribution company at home), (2) *Their Way* (use a more ritual, formal,

longer-time-frame MC appropriate to their understanding of
Japanese organizational culture), (3) *Compromise* between the
two, or (4) *develop an IMC* tailored to the ecology of this
specific negotiation. If they selected the last strategy, they
would need to assess the characteristics of this ecology.

Keeping matters simple, let's say that this assessment
singled out the following key ecological characteristics:

1. The possibility that the Japanese company is itself
   seeking the most useful strategy and may or may not be
   sophisticated enough internationally to have considered
   the need for an IMC.

2. Neither the Americans nor the Japanese speak the
   others' language adequately to support an important
   negotiation so both teams have hired their own
   interpreter.

3. Because of its financial difficulties, the American company can only afford to keep its personnel in Japan and
   away from other tasks for a limited time. Additionally,
   the likelihood of a subsequent visit being judged cost-
   effective by their CEO is slim. The Japanese company, of
   course, is not under such contraints.

4. The Japanese personnel are unlikely to be comfortable
   with making decisions during a face-to-face meeting,
   especially if they feel time constraints.

5. The American personnel are likely to be suffering from
   jet lag and ecoshock for the duration of the negotiation.

6. The Japanese personnel most likely will require some opportunity to develop a sense of trust for the Americans
   prior to any formal agreement especially since they, too,
   are aware of the Americans' financial difficulties.

7. Immediate communication between the American
   negotiators and their head office in Los Angeles is likely
   to be difficult because of time-zone differences.

An IMC appropriate to this short list of ecological
characteristics might include the following perceptions
numbered correspondingly:

1. It would be useful for the companies to engage in some
   initial dialogue describing some of the ecological constraints under which they must negotiate, their desire to
   be responsive to each others' constraints, and suggestions as to procedures that might be appropriate to
   those constraints. This dialogue could occur via a tradi-

tional exchange of letters or a preliminary visit or, more creatively, teleconferencing.

2. Since it is difficult to communicate well enough through interpreters to support either the Americans' adversarial bargaining strategy or the indirectness and subtlety of the Japanese style, the negotiation must be much more straightforward in making and responding to offers.

3. It will be necessary for the negotiation to come to some formal conclusion within the time constraints of the American company but also allowing for the more time-consuming decision-making process of the Japanese. Planning a couple of relatively short trips rather than one extended trip might be both more cost-effective and allow for more flexible decision-making time lines.

4/5. Rather than concentrated, day-long negotiating sessions, it would be more effective to have shorter sessions interspersed with other activities (the Americans' time constraints notwithstanding). This procedure would both allow the Japanese personnel the opportunity for discussion and consensual decision making outside the formal meetings and allow the Americans to adjust better to jet lag and ecoshock.

6. It would be useful if some of the above breaks involved at least *formal* socializing opportunities between Japanese and American personnel. This would allow, among other things, the Japanese to develop some sense of the "character" or "trustworthiness" of the Americans.

7. Since communication with the home office may be difficult, it would be necessary that the American negotiating team have a great deal of discretion in committing their company to terms of an agreement. This might mean their team would need to include personnel at the highest administrative level—a tactic that can have other benefits as well.

Additionally, it would be necessary for the Americans to have quick access to the information they require to negotiate an attractive contract including whatever legal counsel may be necessary. Since the team cannot return to the home office to get the information, it would be useful to have a home office support staff in close contact with the team and the adequacy of communication media should be a major consideration in the selection of accommodation and negotiation facilities.

This case illustrates possible IMC development in response to a *minimal* number of ecological characteristics. Other potential task-specific concerns could be the appropriateness of including the marketing manager on the American team (women are infrequently involved in contract negotiation in Japan) and whether the firm's attorney should be present or left in good contact back home (in many cultures, the presence of attorneys is viewed with suspicion). At the organizational culture level, there would be ample justification for leaving both at home, but from an IMC perspective, that might not necessarily be the case. It could well be that the presence of the attorney could be negotiated into the IMC as part of the preliminary groundwork between the two companies. It could also be that in the entertainment industry Japanese are used to working with women and her presence might add to, rather than detract from, the negotiation. Including her on the team might, however, impact the perceived appropriateness within the IMC of different socializing opportunities—a hotel cocktail lounge versus a *karaoke* bar, for instance. An IMC associated with a very different kind of business context is illustrated next.

---

### Case Illustration K

Perhaps no type of organization engages in as many international "assignments" as an international airline, and perhaps in no other do the assignments play such a central role in business. Anyone who has flown much internationally over the last several years recognizes that a "flight culture" has developed that is broadly shared among both passengers and flight crew. This culture is evidenced on almost any international flight on almost any airline. It is based on ecological similarities between most international flights such as the following:

- Restricted storage space and seating room leads to limits placed on the number and size of carry-on luggage and tolerance for violations of personal space. Passengers must accept sitting, eating, watching movies, and even sleeping much more intimately than their relationship would generally allow outside this ecology. Interestingly, this ecological charactistic is similar to that encountered on elevators. However, on them, the very short duration allows people to cope effectively with the greater *physical* intimacy by reducing *psychological* intimacy through diverted eye contact and discontinued conversation. On long international flights, that is difficult. "Flight culture" allows for an increased psychological intimacy manifested in eye contact and both the frequency and topics of conversation.

- The limited availability of food and drink leads to acceptance of very reduced menus (often only two selections) for each meal with the type of food dependent commonly on the culture of the point of embarkation. Further, the crew/passenger ratio (much lower outside of business or first class than the server/customer ratio in a restaurant) and limited aisle space leads to accepting food and drink sequentially rather than simultaneously.

- The relatively long duration of international flights leads to more emphasis placed both on entertainment (movies, radio, games, magazines) and comfort (it's OK to loosen clothes and remove shoes). Further, the selection of clothes should be based less on initial stylishness than on appropriateness to the cool, dry air and their "stylishness" after sleeping in them.

- Most international flights have passengers from a variety of countries speaking a variety of primary languages. That ecological characteristic leads to the necessity for "official" information (on menus, announcements, and safety instructions) to be presented both in the primary language of the majority of passengers as well as some "international" language (usually English).

- The fact that air travel continues to cause anxiety to many passengers and crew leads to some restriction on topics of conversation: talking about airline crashes, hijackings, or bombs is frowned upon; even reading the safety instruction card in the seat pocket or checking for the life jacket under the seat should be done surreptitiously.

Beyond these ecological similarities to which *any* "flight culture" must respond (and thus its basis at the organizational level) are a range of differences that sets one particular flight apart from others: that give it its own character. If the culture is to constitute an IMC, then it must be tailored to these *differences* as well:

- If the particular flight has multiple stopovers across multiple time zones, then the passengers are literally living at different times of day in the same place and much more flexibility in mealtimes and who receives them is required. And because sleep is more important then entertainment, the former should be catered to even if it disrupts the latter.

- The culture of the majority of the passengers or the crew or the culture at the destination will often impact a particular "flight culture" in a variety of ways from the types of drinks served to the general ambience. A flight with Australian holidaymakers requires quite a different IMC from that of French businesspersons.

- There may on occasions be incompatibility between passengers (crying babies with sleeping businesspersons) or crew requiring special treatment. Families with babies may have to be treated very differently.

- Unanticipated weather and turbulence problems may force major changes in everything from the freedom to move around to the timing of the meals to the topics of conversation, as, of course, can unexpected mechanical problems.

On a recent trip to Singapore, my plane was delayed in Hong Kong for *one* hour by a minor mechanical problem. To deal with this particular unanticipated ecological characteristic, the crew encouraged passengers to leave the plane and walk around and provided free soda and cocktails. On a previous trip form Montreal to Seattle, my airline lost an engine, had to make an emergency landing in Chicago, and was delayed for *five* hours. Initially the crew refused to let anybody off the plane and didn't provide any refreshments. Their reason—it was against company policy. That's the difference between doing business in an IMC and in an organizational culture, between good business and bad business. China Airlines calls each trip an "encounter"—that's what "individualized" service means.

## The Lifetime of an IMC

The *lifetime* of an IMC is limited chiefly to the duration of the task. An IMC could be resurrected for similar tasks on future assignments, but usually the task ecologies will have changed enough that significantly altered perceptions would be necessary. There might, for instance, be new people and different resources available or a very different political climate.

An IMC must extend beyond the duration of a task or assignment, however, when it involves treaty or contractual agreements with future obligations for the participants. In these cases at least those perceptions relevant to fulfilling the obligations must be carried over until the obligations have been met: agreements, for example, on who will absorb the increased price of materials in a contract for a Taiwanese company to provide video recorders to the Australian government. But, then, agreements are not always carried over and business may fail: perceptions of obligations change and come into conflict. For instance, the perceptions of the United States and Soviet Union in arms reduction talks with respect to the scope of surveillance may subsequently change markedly with changes in both political climate and developments in arms and surveillance technology.

It should be stressed also that an IMC, like any other culture, is *not* static. It is continuously transformed as the participants attempt to improve it and in response to inevitable ecological change. This transformation would, of course, be most prominent in IMCs of longer duration such as those in extended treaty negotiations.

### The Members of an IMC

The members of an IMC include chiefly the task participants: those on an international assignment and the host country nationals with whom they are doing business. It is they who must negotiate an appropriate IMC and then work within it. But, as with the lifetime, treaty or contractual obligations may necessitate extending membership to others that are involved in monitoring or fulfilling these obligations. The perceptions that facilitate completing the task must be at least accepted—if not preferred—by those assuming the obligations in the home office. Those back home in the goverment or corporation or university must be at least passive members of that IMC. Since they typically are not involved in its development and are often far from the scene, a major communication—if not "selling"—responsibility by those *on* the scene is highlighted. The same, of course, must be said for the host country participant and the organization to which he or she must report.

## HOW SPECIFIC IMCs ARE DEVELOPED

IMCs can be *adopted* in their entirety from previous IMCs with which the participants have experience, *adapted* from such IMCs, *provided* by others in IMC networks, or *created* for the specific assignment. In all cases, the key underlying process must essentially be one of negotiation between the participants. They must arrive at a basic agreement on a culture that specifies the way their task is to be done. This culture must be compatible with their capabilities, if not their preferences. And then they must proceed to do business within it until they complete their task successfully, give up to try again some other way, or give up forever. All three of these occur frequently.

Even in the case in which an IMC is created to complete a specific task, the perceptions and associated behaviors should *not be new* to the particpants. If they were, they would be unpracticed. And that would largely defeat the advantage of the IMC strategy over the others described previously. Recall that these others are flawed by the necessity of someone having to learn someone else's way of doing business. Perceptions in a newly created IMC need to be taken from those the participants have used in the past with other tasks and with which they *are* practiced. For example, we may not be used to negotiating a contract using the elaborated language and perspective sharing that may be necessary in an IMC. But we may be good at using such language when discussing budgeting with the Accounting Department and such perspective sharing when recruiting new personnel. That experience can then be called on when negotiating a contract on an international assignment. A key to developing an IMC, then, is *creativity in selecting and applying previously learned skills to the new task ecology.* A key to training then becomes *showing the participants the relevance of these skills to the tasks they are likely to face on an international assignment.*

Creativity in negotiating specific IMCs is critical in another sense. As Zartman and Berman state,

> Zero-sum perceptions are characteristic of conflict before it becomes the subject of negotiation; the secret of negotiation is to change that perception and in the process to change the stakes into items that can be used to benefit both parties.

The most positive way of bringing about negotiations is to show the other party the possibilities of creative solutions.[10]

Similarly, Copeland and Griggs state that:

> Home or abroad, negotiating is not a game requiring mere skill but an art requiring forethought, imagination and strategy as well as skill. Whether bargaining for a copper pot in an Egyptian *souk* or negotiating an arms deal with a foreign government, it has less to do with overcoming an adversary than with creating a new picture of reality that is acceptable from two different points of view. If negotiating must be likened to a game, it is a game of perspective.[11]

In their review of the characteristics of *successful* international conflict management, Shaefer and Collen also stress the importance of continuing to provide creative, alternative solutions that meet the needs of all participants.[12]

Negotiating IMCs involves both *motivation* and *competence*. At least in the *exchange* context of assignments, motivation may be the least problematic. I recall sitting in the bar of a luxury international hotel in Hong Kong watching groups of businessmen come in after the day's negotiations and *energetically* discuss what needed to be done better tomorrow. One group of four or five Australians comes vividly to mind literally grabbing the cocktail waitress (!) and interrogating her on what alternative ways of doing things might work better in Hong Kong than what they had apparently done earlier that day. They had plenty of *motivation*! What their organization obviously hadn't done was *competently* prepare them by providing them with some better alternatives.

---

10. Zartman & Berman. *The practical negotiator*, pp. 13, 70.

11. Copeland, L., & Griggs, L. (1985). *Going international: How to make friends and deal effectively in the global marketplace*. New York: Random House, p. 73.

12. Shaefer, S. L., & Collen, A. (1986). Characteristics of successful methods of international conflict management. Unpublished paper presented at the First International Conference on Conflict Resolution and Peace Studies, Suva, Fiji.

Druckman suggests that in international negotiations, much of the difficulty in competently charting direction and defining issues in ways amenable to solution is due to the *high stress* often associated with them.[13] Conference tension, time pressures, the consequences of failure, performance evaluation measures, and unexpected actions by opponents are common sources of this stress. He discusses evidence that stress leads to hostility and simplistic perceptual, cognitive, and group structuring.

Negotiating IMCs is made more complex because the definition of a task, the perception of what constitutes the appropriate parameters of a task, and the attitudes toward a task are often culturally different. Thus for some, dinner at a fine restaurant might be within the parameters of a decision-making task, while for others, it is a separate, social activity. For some, it may be perceived as an opportunity; for others, as a chore. The ease of IMC negotiation may in part reflect the similarity between the participants in how the tasks themselves are perceived.

Blake and Mouton present a formalized approach to international negotiation relevant to developing IMCs. Their approach is based on the principle that:

> people can recognize and generally agree on a model of the ideal or soundest relationship against which to view the actual situation . . . . [The approach] is designed to surface, analyze, and permit consensus to be reached on the elements for both the soundest relationship, the actual relationship, and joint commitment steps in order to close the gap between.[14.]

The product of their approach is a list of characteristics of the model that have to be agreed to. They present a case study of an American-Chinese airplane contract negotiation in which the list included communications, trust and respect, and scheduling as the important characteristics. In terms of an IMC strategy,

---

13. Druckman, D. (1977). Social-psychological approaches to the study of negotiation. In D. Druckman (Ed.), *Negotiations: Social-psychological perspectives*. Beverly Hills, CA: Sage.

14. Blake, R. R., & Mouton, J. S. (1986). *Occidental-oriental intercultural conflict solving*. Austin, TX: Scientific Methods, pp. 3-4.

this list would constitute the key dimensions of perception in this specific IMC.

A somewhat different perspective on IMC development can be derived from Singer's concept of a "unique personal culture" and his application of it to international negotiation. He suggests that everyone has a unique culture because they represent a unique combination of "identity groups" (doctors, accountants, engineers, journalists, etc.) with whom they share perceptions. In the terms used in Chapter 2, everyone has a "unique set of networks" and thus "different perceptions of the world and how to do business in it." Persons from quite different national cultures may have identity groups—and thus some perceptions— in common. This implies that some IMCs may not be so much *consciously-developed* as the product of the *fortuitous overlapping* of relevant components of the participants' personal cultures:

> the reason they are relatively so successful is that the people with whom they must communicate most intensely day to day do share a good number of cultures in common with them. Thus many of their most important communications internationally may not have been nearly as intercultural as one might have expected them to be.[15]

To the degree that such is the case, screening on identity group matching criteria might increase the frequency with which successful IMCs occur: making them more *planned* then *fortuitous*.

## THE QUALITY OF AN IMC

The "bottom line" of quality for an IMC is of course, *Does it work?* Does it get the task completed acceptably? There are, however, some more intermediate criteria. For instance, Zartman and Berman specify several characteristics that a useful *formula* must have regardless of the specific perceptions it contains.[16]

---

15. Singer, M. R. (1987). *Intercultural communication: A perceptual approach.* Englewood Cliffs, NJ: Prentice Hall, pp. 230–231.

16. Zartman & Berman. *The practical negotiator.*

Some of these can be applied to IMCs as criteria of their quality. For example,

- The *comprehensiveness* of the IMC in including at least the minimum range of perceptions necessary to complete the task.
- The *balance* of the IMC in terms of addressing fairly the constraints and objectives of all participants.
- The *flexibility* of the IMC in terms of its responsivity to changes in ecology that occur during the task.
- The *stability* of the IMC in the sense that, while being flexible, it must still maintain an integrity so that participants are not left swimming in ambiguity during transitions or find it replaced all together.

Another criterion would certainly be the *efficiency* of the IMC in terms of the speed with which the task can be completed successfully. This efficiency would be directly related to the degree to which the IMC specifies ways to do business that are compatible with skills that the participants *already possess*. This would limit the requisite time in education or training needed to build *new* skills.

## SKILLS IN DEVELOPING IMCs

To the extent that developing IMCs is the optimal strategy for doing business consistently successfully on international assignments, the skills associated with that development become essential for such assignments. Both the approach taken in this book and that taken by researchers in practical intelligence identify the central role of a skill which ties an effective problem-solving strategy to an awareness of the ecology. I suggest that this skill is primarily *perceptual* and label it a **sense of presence**. Additionally, because international business most commonly involves mutual (rather than individual) problem solving, the importance of **social skills** to develop and maintain relationships is apparent. Because of the likelihood of cultural differences **communication skills**, particularly in language, ritual, perspective, and agenda matching are required. And to cope with ecoshock **stress-management skills** are important. Together, all four skills provide the type of "skill package" most likely to lead to IMC development and successful international assignments. They are the basis for *inter*cultural as opposed to *cross*-cultural training and are the subject of the next two chapters.

## SOME FINAL NOTES

The *tacit knowledge* of those consistently effective on international assignments can be of two kinds:

1. It can involve the *generic* IMC strategy identified in this chapter: we do business consistently effectively by using a strategy that involves developing IMCs tailored to the ecology of specific tasks we must complete as part of those assignments. This is a strategy for selecting the best *specific* strategy to complete a task.
2. It can involve a *specific* strategy (such as *Our Way* or *Their Way* or *Compromise*) and applying that strategy generally across all tasks and assignments. This letter strategy then becomes a kind of rule of thumb or list of do's and don'ts.

To be consistently effective on international assignments, those with the second kind of tacit knowledge must be *very lucky*. They are lucky because (1) they have adopted (for whatever reason) a specific strategy that *happens* to fit a task ecology and (2) that ecology *happens* to remain stable across time and tasks for them. That same "rule of thumb" may not work for somebody else (or even for them in the future if the ecology changes). But a funny thing happens with rules of thumb: we notice when they work and tend not to notice when they don't! Thus we see a successful businessperson and ask him his "secret." He gives us his rule of thumb (for instance, "always do the critical things *Our Way*"). And we adopt it, or maybe train others in it, or maybe write a book about it.

What we don't see are those who use his rule of thumb and commonly fail. We don't study the failures. We don't ask for their "secret." We assume they are using some *other* ineffectual rule of thumb. We evidence what social science calls a **positive instance bias**. We don't see the covariation between the effectiveness of a strategy and the ecology in which it's used; we don't see the perception-ecology link. So on our own assignments we "always do the critical things *Our Way.*" And we often fail. And we can't figure out why. Or perhaps we're simply left with the humbling, "I must not be very good."

It should also be noted that the IMC strategy presented in this chapter is a *description* of what is necessary to be consistently successful on international assignments. Those who are so *may* not conceptualize their strategy that way. It might not be part of their *tacit knowledge* at all. If asked what they do, they may not describe the strategy in terms reflective of an awareness of the perception-ecology link at the task level. They may even say "I do it their way." But they don't. What they actually do is take *Their Way* into consideration when developing an IMC.

Some other issues should be noted. Developing IMCs involves replacing habitual ways of doing business based on the organizational or nationl culture. But we sometimes—usually at the "wrong" time—revert back to our habits. We reimpose the old ways. This occurs under stress or out of frustration. An IMC does not usually have documentation, institutional support, or historical precedent. As such it can be a very fragile thing. Its development and maintenance relies on sustained good intentions, constant monitoring, and mutual trust.

Further, we must remember that an IMC is shared among the participants, but *developing* it may *not* be *equally* shared. A number of factors may affect who works the hardest. The smart businessperson influences the task in such a way that an IMC develops, with or without the awareness and help of others.

Further still, to participate in IMCs we—at least for a time—must often become a different person. While as indicated earlier some may relish that experience, we do not all wish to be so because of morals, ethics, timidity, inertia, or concern with self-identity. Bribery, lying to maintain harmony, criticizing a superior, accepting responsibility for something not done, not doing something one is responsible for, seducing or being seduced, and sharing tantalizing pleasures with those with power are only hints of the range of such dilemmas. To participate actively in IMCs, we can be confronted with the need to violate important perceptions of our own organizational or national culture. On such occasions doing international business requires *tough* decisions.

Finally, even if we accept the need to dart from one IMC to another like a butterfly, those in our home culture may not be very amused. Many national cultures, for example, discourage long absences from home, exclude women from business, or have prohibitions against alcohol, yet an IMC may involve extended trips, the active participation of women, and our presence at cocktail parties. Most IMCs may be relatively private, but they are rarely secret. Those from *our* own culture may exact a price for our participation in *another*. On such occasions, doing international business requires *sacrifices*.

# A
# SENSE
# OF
# PRESENCE

# Chapter 6

# A PERCEPTUAL SKILL

The first theme of this book is that developing IMCs is the optimal strategy for doing international business consistently effectively, and thus the skills to develop them are essential for successful assignments. As introduced in the previous chapter, I suggest that the central skill is primarily perceptual and label it a **sense of presence**. It is seeing ways for doing business that will work in assignment ecologies. It is a sense of the *necessary*, the *possible*, and the *desirable* in a specific task. It is the international assignment equivalent of "street smarts."

*That is the SECOND THEME of this book.*

When we do business at home we are often much less than 100 percent there—"present"—psychologically. During a meeting, our mind is occupied by things that happened on the way to it, previous meetings, the next one we must go to, characteristics of the people or facility having no relevance to the task at hand, a problem at home, bills to be paid, how tired we feel, the vacation we need, and so forth. That is, we are not "tuned in" to the ecology of the immediate task. Because so much of our business at home is routine and predictable, we don't need to be. We simply do not frequently need that level of presence to function adequately. It would waste precious energy. We can get by on being 25 percent there! At home the relatively stable ecology allows general rules for completing tasks to develop. We need not monitor minor variations in ecology between successive occurrences of a task. Each can be approached habitually and often with success.

But international business is not so routine. It involves *new* ecologies. Because so many of them are *unpredictable* beforehand, we rarely have the opportunity for adequate planning: we must be prepared to "do it on the spot." Because task ecologies so often *change* even as we are "doing it," we need to monitor them continuously. Because there is always the danger—particularly at times of stress or frustration—of falling back on *habits* developed at home and probably ineffective internationally, we need to monitor our own behavior as well. To do business effectively on international assignments, we need to be nearly 100 percent there, 100 percent involved, 100 percent *present!*

What is a sense of presence like? The following unattributed editorial about American politician Jesse Jackson gives some idea:[1]

---

## What is Jesse Jackson's Secret?

It is, I think, that he is totally aware of his surroundings. He listens. He sees. He is alive to everything, sensitive to the words, the sights and the people within his range. That may not seem like much. But, in my experience, it is very rare in people of power, especially in professional politicians. It may be that they are so self-centered that they don't notice what is happening around them. Some may condition themselves to dull their perceptions and thus their human reflexes. Spontaneous reaction is generally considered a political liability . . . . Careful. Better to handle this one on automatic pilot.

I have never seen Jackson on automatic pilot. The man is alive. I also never saw him lose the audience at a debate or joint appearance, beginning with his first one in New Hampshire in January 1984. He was expected to make a fool of himself that day. . . . But he carried the afternoon. He was physically different from the other candidates. His body movements were open and loose, his head and eyes moving with interest toward his opponents. There was only one other man like him on the stage that day, the moderator, Phil Donahue.

It was the same Tuesday at the *Daily News* Forum. When Dukakis began his final statement by saying that his cousin, Olympia Dukakis, had won an Academy Award, Jackson broke into a smile. All right, the man's cousin made it, and I know him. Albert Gore, next to Jackson, maintained the face of a man slightly ill, as if Dukakis were spreading more germs. When Dukakis finished, Jackson smiled and began to applaud. We're all up here together. After two claps, Gore took notice and began to tap his hands. I wouldn't be surprised if he washed them as soon as he got off the stage.

---

1. Unattributed editorial in *Sunday Star-Bulletin & Adviser*, Honolulu, Hawaii, April 17, 1988.

In front of an audience, Jackson has a sense of presence: he sees the situation and responds appropriately. On international assignments we cannot rely on "automatic pilot" either. It's not programmed for those assignments. I recall a recent bus ride from my hotel to nearby Narita airport near Tokyo in which careful observation of a passenger's attire to infer a destination, opportune use of a routine security check to note the passport and occupation of another passenger, and an appropriate response to eye contact initiated by still another led to three apparently good professional contacts in about 25 minutes for a diplomat from Taipei. *He* had a sense of presence. I was in the meantime being "guided" by my automatic "airport bus" program with no such outcome. Nor did the American couple with us on their way to China fare any better—they were paying so much *attention* to their luggage that they missed their terminal.

Unlike *attention* which involves a *narrow* focus on one specific characteristic of the task ecology (the safety of that lug-

---

## Case Illustration L

The International Catholic Migration Commission has the contract to offer English as a second language, work orientation, and cultural orientation for Indochinese refugees bound for the United States at the Philippine Refugee Processing Center in Bataan. Program administrators and supervisors are comprised of Americans, Filipinos, and those from a smattering of other countries. The trainers, themselves, are all Filipino. This results in the rather curious situation in that those providing training in American culture have for the most part never been to the United States. This irony is not missed by most trainers—nor probably most refugees—but several trainers have found ways to deal successfully with this ecological characteristic of their assignment.

One trainer who appears particularly effective—let's call him Alberto—has noted that the center is quite frequently toured by various Americans for a variety of reasons. Thus during training Alberto attempts to maintain an awareness, not only of the activities within the training room itself, but also the foot traffic outside the room. He has become quite adept at recruiting American passersby to spend a minute or two giving his trainees exposure to American perspectives as well as his own. He has a sense of presence.

gage or a speaker at a luncheon, for instance), *a sense of presence* involves a *broad* focus on all potentially relevant characteristics. We require a sense of presence when driving a car. We must be aware of the road, road conditions, other traffic, the mechanical state of our car, our driving capability, where we are, where we are going, alternative ways to get there, traffic regulations, and so forth. Too narrow a focus on any one of these ecological characteristics will interfere with our performance. We must be aware of them all—any one of them alone or in combination may place a critical demand on us. And the pattern is unpredictable. Too much "attention" on the centerline and we'll crash!

A sense of presence is necessary when the task ecology is new, different, or changing, and we must appropriately develop or adjust an MC or an IMC. It's meaning is close to that of the more colloquial "presence of mind," which *Webster's*[2] defines as "self-control so maintained in an emergency, in danger, or in an embarrassing situation that one can say or do the right thing." "Presence" is defined by *Webster's* as "the state of being in one place and not elsewhere." This is, literally at least, a *spatial* definition. There is also a *temporal* aspect described by Ornstein's[3] definition of "present": "This is the time of our immediate contact of the world, a very short, continually changing, fading away, forever being replaced by a new NOW."

We all have had experiences in which the world seemed more vivid, more immediate, more real; when we were more aware of our surroundings and who we are; when we simply felt more alive! Perhaps it was like the wonder of a child who sees something for the first time with no expectations. These moments are sometimes called "peak experiences," though they can be a bit less dramatic than that. They are *not* abstract. They occur at a real time and a real place: at the sight of an owl alighting on a branch against a flaming red sunset, at the sound of frogs on a hot, sticky night, during combat or overtime in a basketball game, the first days with a new lover, our first business trip to Singapore or New York. For different people—different times and different places. But

2. *Webster's third new world dictionary.* (1981). Springfield, MA: Merriam-Webster.

3. Ornstein, R. E. (1972). *The psychology of consciousness.* New York: Penguin.

we've all had the experience! Those are times we've had a sense of presence. And most of us long for more.

The sense of presence is like blinking and suddenly, perhaps briefly, *seeing* the world clearly.[4] Our culture focuses our attention on certain characteristics of the world and that focus is important for us. But it glosses over the remainder. A sense of presence occurs when we blink, and the gloss is swept away.

While such experiences are ordinarily infrequent, they are not particularly so on international assignments. One week into an international assignment can feel like months because we've encountered so many new ecologies and been so aware of them all. The stop-the-world experiences,[5,6] the ecoshock, so common on such assignments can produce the proper level of arousal to trigger a sense of presence. It is the source of the intensity that makes those assignments so appealing and later brings on the longing to "return international." What we on international assignments must learn to do is take advantage of the sense of presence triggered by those experiences and refine it to the needs of doing business. That is the most noticeable trait of an American executive who concluded the first U.S. acquisition of a Japanese company in his industry: when doing business internationally, he is "alive"; between business deals he is usually in the same routine as the rest of us. Another professional successful internationally seems to come alive principally on his assignments. Back home his demeanor is more tuned to hibernation, stoked only by his longing for the next trip. Observing him doing business at home, we would never guess at his overseas effectiveness.

The impact of having a sense of presence on doing business is that, rather than doing it in a manner based on habit, custom, stereotype, or preoccupation with the outcome, we instead base it on our awareness of the ecologically *necessary*, *possible*, and *desirable* in the task at hand. In other words, what *must* be done, what *can* be done, and what would *best* be done in this task ecology? While past customs and future goals are certainly part

---

4. Castaneda, C. (1972). *Journey to Ixtlan*. New York: Simon & Schuster.

5. Ibid.

6. Murray, G. (1977). The inner side of cross-cultural interaction. In D. Batchelder & E. G. Warner (Eds.), *Beyond experience*. Washington, D.C.: Society for Intercultural Education, Training and Research.

of that ecology, they are by no means the only part. It is only through a sense of presence that IMCs can be developed that are, in fact, tailored to the constantly changing task ecologies in which international business is done.

## THE NECESSARY

One aspect of the sense of presence is an *ecological awareness*: an awareness of all the relevant characteristics of the task ecology, an awareness of the **necessary**. This includes awareness of the space, the temperature, the light, the sounds, the color, the texture, the sensations from our own bodies, the people around us, our relationships to them, the purpose of being together with them, and so forth. It includes awareness of all, or at least most, of the ecological characteristics that typify international assignments, that differentiate one from another, and that are associated with a specific task. A sense of presence, for instance, would commonly involve:

- A *sense of place*—What are the characteristics of the country, the city, the hotel, and the meeting room that we are in? What are their constraints? What are their advantages? What is their spatial relationship to other places? How do we get between them? What are some alternatives?

- A *sense of time*—Where is this country historically? Where are the people coming from? Where are they going? What time is it in their day and their life? How important is time to them? Where does this task fit into a sequence of tasks? How much time is this task going to take for them? How much time do they need? How much time do they have? And the same for *us*.

- A *sense of people*—Who are these people? What is their culture? What is their language? What are they like? Why are they that way? What are they good at? What have been their experiences? What do they expect? What do they want? What is their mission? Why are

they doing business with us? What support do they need
to do the business well? And the same for *us*.

- A *sense of task*—What resources are required? What
resources are available? What decisions must be made?
Who must make them? What facilities are required?
What are available? What are the task objectives? What
are the sequences of things? What are the consequences
of failure? What are the side effects of success? How
is it functionally related to other tasks?

Samovar, Porter, and Jain suggest similarly the importance of
the awareness of "timing, physical setting, and custom on human
interaction."[7] Steele stresses the importance of a "sense of
place" about the physical setting in which tasks are completed.[8]
Hall discusses the necessity of learning "situational dialects and
frames" in a manner directly related to a sense of place and "action chains" in a manner related to a sense of time.[9] We must
be aware of the situational context that gives meaning to the actions of ourselves and others, and we must be aware that those
actions have a place in a sequence of actions. Like a dance, the
steps have meaning only as part of the situation and the sequence.
And, as we know, dances are culturally very different!

A sense of presence encompasses an ecological awareness
of all or most of these things. It is unlikely to involve attention
to each *individually*, however. It is more *holistic*. In other words,
breaking down the sense of presence into a sense of people, place,
time, and task and the separate characteristics of each is done
here for *descriptive* purposes only: to aid our grasp of the concept. It is, however, unlikely to be *experienced* in this analytical
way. In fact, to try to do so may well hinder its development:
analysis takes us away from the immediacy of the experience;
it produces *more* gloss than it removes.

Thus the sense of presence is more *intuitive* than analytical.
As expressed by Zartman and Berman,

---

7. Samovar, L. A., Porter, R. E., & Jain, N. C. (1981). *Understanding intercultural communication*. Belmont, CA: Wadsworth, p. 205.

8. Steele, F. (1986). *Making and managing high-quality workplaces: An
organizational ecology*. New York: Teachers College Press.

9. Hall, E. T. (1981). *Beyond culture*. Garden City, NY: Anchor Press.

many [diplomats] believe that if negotiation does require some special skills these come through an acquired "feel of things" and are beyond capture and transmission as rules and theories.[10]

Or as Hoy and Boulton warn, even domestically students may be conditioned by the

logical, sequential, task-oriented, decision-making process generally recommended in management education literature. If such conditioning occurs, [they] may be ill-prepared for comprehending the more intuitive styles of problem solving which are required as they progress upward in organizational hierarchies.[11]

On an international assignment the character of the task ecology and the necessary, possible, and desirable in it is more *perceived*, than analyzed. That is why I call it a *sense* of presence.

On the other hand, there may be a few ecological characteristics that *are* attended to separately. They may act as *cues* to elicit IMC development. Some participants in international business may have implicit theories about different types of ecologies and the perceptions which are appropriate for doing business in them. They then are on the "lookout" for cues as to which type of ecology they are faced with. Certain ecological characteristics that are more obvious or, through experience, more informative of the ecological type may then be *central cues* for predicting the ecology. We may, for instance, find from experience that slight eccentricities in our host's dress (a differently colored tie, tinted lenses, or unusual cufflinks) cue either an innovative personality or flexible cultural expectations or both in an ecology and suggest that IMC development might proceed rather quickly. Or we may have learned that the presence of news media puts our hosts on guard, tends to make them more conservative, and suggests that development of an innovative IMC must be approached with caution and patience. The development of such

---

10. Zartman, I. W., & Berman, M. R. (1982). *The practical negotiator.* New Haven, CT: Yale University Press, p. 1.

11. Hoy, F., & Boulton, W. R. (1983). Problem-solving styles of students— Are educators producing what business needs? *Collegiate News and Views,* Spring, p. 17.

theories and identification of good cues may be one important pathway to a sense of presence. They may be part of that *tacit knowledge* of those consistently successful internationally.

## THE POSSIBLE

Awareness of the task ecology is an aspect of a sense of presence, but not all of it. Within the context of this awareness, we must see which of a range of ways of doing things should work. Awareness of a broad range of alternatives from which to select is, then, another important aspect of a sense of presence. It is an awareness of the **possible**. It is important because our limited range of habitual ways (based on our organizational or national culture) is unlikely to be sufficient in the international ecologies we face. Hoy and Boulton suggest that

> Perhaps the greatest contribution that can be made by management educators would be to increase student awareness of alternative problem-solving styles and the contingencies under which these styles are most appropriate.[12]

Internationally we must be aware of lots of *our ways* and their ways and other ways. We need to be creative. Not necessarily creative in identifying original ways of doing business, but creative in applying to the task at hand ways of doing business common in other tasks. That awareness may come from our own experience or the experience of others. Expanding it is a realistic and useful objective of orientation and training in preparation for international assignments, as we will see in Chapters 8 and 9. An awareness of the ecology without awareness of alternatives for dealing with it produces a sense of "clarity and impotence" and the common consequence is *frustration*.

## THE DESIRABLE

The third aspect of a sense of presence is seeing within a broad range of alternatives for doing business those that are appropriate to the ecology. It is an awareness of the **desirable**. For example,

---

12. Ibid., p. 21.

a common characteristic of international assignments is that our language is not the primary language of other participants. In such cases, we have to be aware of difficulties they may have understanding us (the necessary), be aware of a range of ways for dealing with those difficulties (the possible), and see in that range some that are ecologically appropriate (the desirable). Speaking more slowly with lots of breaks and patiently letting them complete their "rehearsed" dialogue without interruption could be such ways.

Seeing an appropriate alternative involves specifying those perceptions on how to do business that fit the task ecology: *that could comprise an IMC.* Zartman and Berman, for instance, suggest that skillful negotiators must "think of alternate solutions" and then arrive at an acceptable *formula* for negotiation based essentially on a trial and error process.[13] The chosen alternative must be tailored to the task, the people involved, and all other important characteristics of that ecology. That is why awareness of a broad range of alternatives mentioned earlier is so important. If the range is too narrow, there may not be an appropriate one to choose.

Seeing an appropriate alternative may in some instances be based on *trial and error* as Zartman and Berman suggest. But that requires a number of repetitions of similar task ecologies so that we can make mistakes and learn from them. It may also be based on *past experience* with task ecologies and ways of doing business that work well together. The career-long experience of "old hands" is invaluable in this respect—if a sense of presence has been part of that experience. We may be able to use an awareness of the *experience of others.* They represent a wealth of encounters that no one person could ever match. But how different are those people from us, and how does that difference alter the task ecology? And how accurate is their description, or our understanding, of what they did? We must be careful. Or we may *figure it out* using our understanding of the ways of doing business that should work with particular ecologies given our "theories" of business, people, resources, effectiveness, and so forth. This involves a mixture of analytical thinking as well as perception. The question then becomes: How good are our theories and how quick is our analysis?

---

13. Zartman & Berman. *The practical negotiator,* p. 85.

Once we have identified and implemented an alternative, it is important to monitor its effectiveness continuously. This involves more than just seeing if it's working but determining why or why not? Was our ecological awareness too narrow? Were we aware of an insufficiently broad range of alternatives? Was the wrong one chosen? Was it performed poorly? We must, of course, do it! And doing it may be difficult. If it's new to us, we need to gain whatever performance skills are required. Remember that the skills associated with our habitual ways of doing business have taken a career to develop. We aren't going to learn and perform new ones overnight. Even "speaking more slowly and arranging frequent breaks" can be tough if it's not our way. That's why seeing an *appropriate* alternative in part means one associated with skills already acquired in other contexts. To the degree that it isn't, practice, patience, and lower performance expectations are usually required.

Thus a sense of presence involves identifying ways of doing business that meet the criteria of the necessary, possible, and

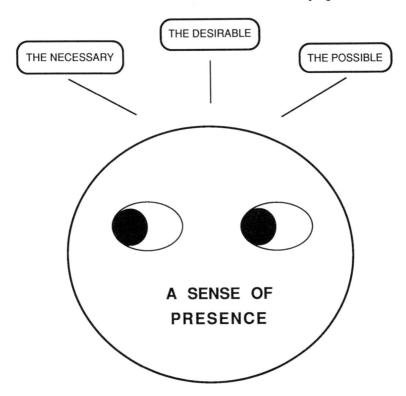

**Figure 6.1**   A Sense of Presence

desirable in the task ecology. These three aspects are summarized in Figure 6.1. Once a way of doing business has been identified, the participants must do it and monitor how it's working. That monitoring may or may not be useful for the task at hand (we may get only one try at it on a given assignment), but it can be very important for seeing how best to do business on subsequent assignments. We need to learn from our present assignment how to be more effective on our next one!

## SOME RELATED APPROACHES

There are several concepts described in the international literature related to a sense of presence but in one important way or another are distinct from it. They may focus on a much narrower range of ecological characteristics (only cultural differences, for instance) or focus on perceptions of the ecology but not ways to deal with it. A brief look at a few of them should help to clarify what a sense of presence is and isn't.

### Stereotyping

Whenever we approach a task domestically or internationally, we approach it with a package of expectations based on our perceptions of the task and the people involved. That is simply good preparation for the task. As we have seen, domestically our expectations are most commonly confirmed. When our expectations for people are based on their *social category* (culture, nationality, race, ethnicity, sex, age, profession, and so forth) rather than on their being unique individuals, the process is often called **stereotyping**. Particularly internationally, we may need to rely on such a process because we simply do not have much information about them as individuals.

Stereotyping provides us with at least some basis for predicting what is and isn't likely to be appropriate in doing business with somebody that we otherwise have no experience with. There is commonly at least some "kernel of truth" in our stereotypes.[14] Certain positive stereotypes such as those from another

---

14. Allport, G. E. (1954). *The nature of prejudice*. New York: Doubleday.

culture being friendly, intelligent, or businesslike may facilitate our initial willingness to interact with them and increase the positivity of that interaction.[15] So stereotypes *can* be useful.

But if our stereotypes are inaccurate, if our perceptions of the characteristics of those in a culture are not sufficiently representative, then using them as the basis for doing business can lead us far astray. Part of a sense of presence must be to determine quickly the *accuracy* of our stereotypes as we actually interact with people from another culture and *refine* them as necessary. But it must go beyond that: we must see the ways in which the particular people with whom we are doing business are *unique*, or not well characterized by our stereotype, however accurately it reflects the culture otherwise.

On international assignments quickly refining stereotypes and identifying the uniqueness of those with whom we are interacting is particularly important because most stereotypes are derived from observations of people *in their ecology*. Even if such stereotypes accurately describe them at home, they may not be useful at all in describing them in an international business ecology—where we will be working with them! We all know how people change outside their normal environment—away at school, on vacation, during a convention, or in a nightclub. We can all act differently when the ecological contraints are different. International assignments provide just such an occasion. As mentioned previously, it may be in such assignments that individual characteristics are better predictors of behavior than culture. We may find the person we are doing business with acts very different from our stereotype—however accurate it may otherwise be of him or her at home.

Determining the accuracy of our stereotypes can be difficult because they often have a *self-fulfilling* nature: if we perceive someone to have a particular attribute, we will behave toward them as if they do, and our behavior may cause them to manifest that attribute. For example, if we feel someone is friendly, we act friendly toward them, they are more likely to be friendly to us— and the stereotype is fulfilled. If we expect a place to be boring, and we stay in our hotel and do not actively explore what it has

---

15. Bond, M. H. (1986). Mutual stereotypes and the facilitation of interactions across cultural lines. *International Journal of Intercultural Relations, 10*, 259–276.

to offer, it *is* boring—and the stereotype is fulfilled. This effect can occur across a wide range of stereotypes (about others' intelligence, competence, motivation, and so forth) and profoundly affect our ability to refine them.

Stereotypes are also difficult to refine because of our tendency to perceive *counterinstances* of them (cases in which they are refuted by our experience) as "exceptions." Upon encountering someone who does not conform to our stereotype, we commonly say something like, "People from that culture are like this or that. My host isn't. But, of course, he's an *exception*." This process can lead to all real experience with people from a culture failing to stimulate refinement of a stereotype. Every exception is viewed as just that—an exception—and the stereotype remains intact.

### Attributions

Triandis also focuses on perceptions of other people, particularly our perception of *their* perception of events.[16] Consistent with social psychological terminology he calls our perceptions **attributions** and his concern is with whether we attribute the same meaning to events as our hosts do. When we do, he labels them **isomorphic attributions**, and he suggests that the skill in making them is basic to effective international interaction. His reasoning is that if we can see the world from their perspective, we are better able to predict how they will act and how they will react to how we might act. He presents an elaborate, perceptually based model within which this skill is embedded. He and his associates have developed a training technique called a **cultural assimilator** or **intercultural sensitizer** designed to teach trainees to make isomorphic attributions with people from specific cultures across a range of tasks.[17] Certainly making isomorphic attributions is an important part of a sense of presence.

Kelley and his colleagues have focused on situations in which attributions are *not* isomorphic (**attribution conflict**) and those in which one or more of the participants are unaware of that con-

---

16. Triandis, H. C. (1975). Culture training, cognitive complexity and interpersonal attitudes. In R. Brislin et al. (Eds.), *Cross-cultural perspectives on learning*. New York: John Wiley.

17. Albert, R. (1983). The intercultural sensitizer or culture assimilator: A cognitive approach. In D. Landis & R. W. Brislin (Eds.), *Handbook of intercultural training*, Vol. 2. New York: Pergamon.

flict (**ignorance of attribution conflict**).[18,19] Applying their work to international assignments, we may see an "international mining" investment, for example, as producing profit for us and jobs for our hosts; our hosts see it as exploitation of their limited natural resources and erosion of their way of life. We may both be aware of the conflict, or one or both of us may be ignorant of the conflict. Attribution conflict frequently leads to an overt argument. Ignorance of attribution conflict leads to a feeling of being "out of synchrony" with one another: participants don't respond to events as expected (because, of course, they don't see the events the same way). Both interfere with doing business effectively, but at least when the participants are aware of conflict they can, if motivated, initiate conflict resolution strategies. In international business the development of an IMC can be seen in part as a response to this awareness.

It is important for a sense of presence, then, to be aware of how our host perceives a task—to make isomorphic attributions. But we also need to be aware of how he or she perceives *our* perception of the task so, if there is attribution conflict, *we* at least are not ignorant of it.

### Empathy

One of the traits most commonly ascribed to those effective internationally is **empathy**.[20,21] Empathy is in part equivalent to making isomorphic attributions, but also implies "feeling what the other feels" and communicating this to them. It's often described as the ability to get into the other person's shoes and see how the world looks and feels to them from there.[22] It's not

---

18. Orvis, B. R., Kelley, H. H., & Butler, D. (1976). Attributional conflict in young couples. In J. H. Harvey, W. Ickes, & R. F. Kidd (Eds.), *New directions in attribution research*, Vol 1. Hillsdale, NJ: Erlbaum.

19. Harvey, J. H., Wells, G. C., & Alvarez, M. D. (1978). Attributions in the context of conflict and separation in close relationships. In J. H. Harvey, W. Ickes, & R. F. Kidd (Eds.), *New directions in attribution research*, Vol. 2. Hillsdale, NJ: Erlbaum.

20. Brislin, R. W. (1981). *Cross-cultural encounters: Face-to-face interaction*. New York: Pergamon.

21. Samovar, Porter, & Jain. *Understanding*.

22. Goldstein, R., & Michaels, G. (1985). *Empathy: Development, training, and consequences*. Hillsdale, NJ: Erlbaum.

clear how important this feeling is to a sense of presence which is principally *perceptual*. But the ability to communicate it may help both in letting them know we are aware of their feelings and in motivating them to understand and be positive toward us. That's a big help in developing and maintaining relationships, skills examined in the next chapter.

The ability to empathize is often seen as stemming from shared past experience: we can relate to someone because we have experienced what they have. That is more difficult to achieve on an international assignment because, almost by definition, we share less with our hosts than we do with our colleagues back home. But people that are good at empathy are able to see and feel what the host is, not necessarily because they have had an identical experience, but because they can abstract dimensions of similarity from what might otherwise be a very different experience. Thus someone good at empathy could relate his experiences in combat to a mother's experience of childbirth along a dimension of "anxious anticipation" abstracted from what would otherwise be very different life events. A businessman could relate to his host's pride in the success of her management *team*, even if *his* moments of pride come from *personal* accomplishments alone.

## Generic Problem Solving

The sense of presence is in some respects similar to a generic approach to problem solving as often seen in training variously labeled as social skills,[23] social competence,[24] or environmental competence.[25] It is focused on training people to "learn how to learn" and has recently been applied to international train-

---

23. Singleton, W. T., Spurgeon, P., & Stammers, R. B. (Eds.). (1980). *The analysis of social skill.* New York: Plenum.

24. Argyle, M. (1980). Interaction skills and social competence. In P. Feldman & J. Orford (Eds.), *Psychological problems: The social context.* New York: John Wiley.

25. Steele, F. (1980). Defining and developing environmental competence. In C. P. Alderfer & C. L. Cooper (Eds.), *Advances in experiential social processes.* New York: John Wiley.

ing.[26-28] In this approach effective performance is seen as determined by the demands of the task, the capacity of the performer, and the strategies the performer uses to relate demands to capacities. **Skill** or **competence** is defined as the ability to deal with the environment in an effective and stimulating manner.[29] The central feature in most models is a process in which behavior is continuously monitored and modified as a function of feedback. A typical process would involve

1. Assessing the problem.
2. Identifying a broad range of alternative solutions.
3. Selecting an alternative based on the assessment of the problem and the participant's capabilities and resources.
4. Implementing the selected alternative.
5. Evaluating the effectiveness of the implemented alternative and reexamining the previous steps in light of that evaluation.

In a way this generic approach is the cognitive/analytical counterpart to a more perceptual/intuitive sense of presence. In the foregoing steps (1) is roughly equivalent to awareness of the necessary, (2) to the awareness of the possible, and (3–5) to awareness of the desirable. This generic approach has the benefit (along with a sense of presence) of providing ways of doing business that are effective for *us* given who we are, our personality and resources, and the ecologies in which we most typically find ourselves. It is, however, much more *planned, sequential,* and *analytic* than the sense of presence described here.

The case has already been made that within international assignments there is rarely adequate repetition of specific task

26. Fontaine, G. (1983). Americans in Australia: Intercultural training for the "Lucky Country." In D. Landis & R. W. Brislin (Eds.), *Handbook of intercultural training,* Vol. 3. New York: Pergamon.

27. Hughes-Wiener, G. (1986). The "Learning How to Learn" approach to cross-cultural orientation. *International Journal of Intercultural Relations, 10*(4), 485–505.

28. McCaffery, J. A. (1986). Independent effectiveness: A reconsideration of cross-cultural orientation and training. *International Journal of Intercultural Relations, 10,* 159–178.

29. Steele, F. Defining and developing.

ecologies to allow an iterative feedback process such as this to be useful. However, there *can* be a repetitiveness of organizational ecologies across international assignments, and an approach such as that described here may be usefully applied by an organization in developing a strategy for managing assignments for its personnel. Such a strategy is presented in Chapter 8.

## SOME FINAL NOTES

Thus a sense of presence is the central skill for international assignments. Developing IMCs is what we can do with it to succeed most consistently on those assignments. A sense of presence is more intuitive than analytical, although it has been described analytically here to clarify what it involves. The fact that it is rather intuitive will bother many: those who can't understand or accept things unless they're torn apart and examined. But we must nevertheless accept that we cannot take the intuitive character of an international negotiator out of negotiation, the businessperson out of doing business, or the diplomat out of diplomacy. There is much more there than is ever done, or could be understood, analytically. We will never be able to create a good international negotiator "from scratch." But *if we understand IMCs and a sense of presence, we will be able to take any negotiator, businessperson, or diplomat—so motivated—and make them better.*

Further, it should be noted that if we travel internationally and look for those that are *best*, it is they with a sense of presence that we will *see*. As with Jesse Jackson, they "look different," "look alive"; their eyes are bright. You don't see IMCs. They, remember, are in the minds of the participants. So while developing IMCs is the key strategy for doing business internationally, *it is a sense of presence that most visibly separates the best from the rest.*

Finally, a sense of presence involves a perceptual skill to perceive the world from the host's perspective that facilitates doing business. It is *not* a decision on what to believe. We can appreciate the importance of a beer on a hot day to a beer drinker without having to become one ourselves. That point should be obvious. But people seem to have difficulty distinguishing between perceiving and believing. Training programs are commonly criticized by participants for "promoting" another culture's management system, values, decision-making strategies, and so forth. The question most often asked is: "Why do we have to see or do it their way?" The answer is: We don't, but *it helps to know how they see it and do it if we're going to do business with them.*

# SOCIAL, COMMUNICATION, AND STRESS-MANAGEMENT SKILLS

# Chapter 7

Beyond a sense of presence, other skills are important on international assignments. Several are described in this chapter. They are important because of their relationship to a sense of presence and the development of IMCs and because of their role in coping with ecoshock.

## SOCIAL SKILLS

Social skills are of key importance when doing business internationally.[1] They are particularly important from the perspective of the themes presented thus far in this book. While the focus has been on the psychological manifestation of IMCs in terms of shared perceptions, we must not forget that there is a *social* manifestation as well. These are real people that we do business with on international assignments. We must develop and maintain relationships with our hosts on each task associated with doing business on an assignment. And we must be able to dissolve such relationships amicably when the assignment is completed so that we (or others) can reestablish them in the future if necessary.

Unlike the tasks typically addressed in research on practical intelligence, the development of IMCs involves, at least to some degree, *mutual* problem solving. The concern is not typically with how *I* can best "handle dairy products" as illustrated in Chapter 3, but with how *we* can negotiate a treaty, or *we* can participate in a productive seminar, or *we* can reorganize a subsidiary, or *we* come to an agreement on a plan to reduce the spread of venereal disease in the local community by visiting military personnel. Social skills are necessary *to get people together* and *to bind them together* long enough (during the inevitable cultural conflict) for

---

1. Furnham, A., & Bochner, S. (1986). *Culture shock: Psychological reactions to unfamiliar environments.* New York: Methuen.

IMCs to develop. They are necessary *to keep them together* during the task and *to unbind them* when business is completed.

The *complexity* of our strategies for relationship development, maintenance, and dissolution should not be underestimated. They are among the most difficult things we do in life! They require the most synchronized of behavioral initiatives and responses. The rules governing them are *very* culturally specific. They differ from Sydney to Brisbane, from academic to professional, from 40-year-olds to 30-year-olds. They are so complex that even in our own culture we commonly fail with them. Only a small percentage of the relationships (business or personal) that we wish or need in our lives ever come to fruition—probably a *very* small percentage! And many of our attempts to amicably dissolve those we do establish end in a mess. *And that's at home!*

So how do we do it abroad? How can international relationships ever get initiated, much less maintained? The most useful answer may be that in such cases, the culturally specific rules— that at home serve as a "test" for the appropriateness of the other person as a business or personal partner—are thrown away. If others don't meet the test at home, we don't do business with them. If others don't meet the test abroad, we usually *excuse* them: they, after all, shouldn't be expected to know the rules. But without rules we are swimming in rough seas. The rules have a function. They are, as just mentioned, a screening device: a way to tell if the other person has the same values as we do, is predictable, and is to be trusted. The rules keep participant behaviors in synchrony and help business move along efficiently. Without the rules there is no such screening, there may not be such synchrony, and the development of IMCs can become problematic.

Those skilled at developing, maintaining, and dissolving relationships within organizational or national cultures at home may or may not be equally skilled abroad in different and changing ecologies. A socially skilled person is generally seen as someone who knows the rules or at least exhibits the appropriate behaviors. But in international situations where rules differ and where conformity to them may not be so rigidly required, a very different kind of social skill is necessary.

On an international assignment a socially skilled person is not the one who knows rules well but, rather, is the one who can survive in rough seas by grasping whatever the wind, waves, and tide present him or her with. This skill is so different that quite different kinds of people may have it. The socially skilled person in the home ecology, the person who has learned so well strategies specific to the rules of his or her culture and has practiced them to a routine, may be socially inept in international situations. And vice versa. The successful international professional, who appears so suave at the embassy reception, may be a social "klutz" chatting over beers at a barbecue with neighbors back home!

In international situations well-learned, culture-specific strategies do us little good. Cronen and Shuter stress that

> ... individuals can be assessed as more or less [socially] competent based on comparison of their abilities to the requirements imposed by a particular social system.... minimal competence exists when abilities are less than required by a particular system ... satisfactory competence exists when the individual is enmeshed within the system by a close fit between his or her abilities and the system's requirements ... [and] optimal competence exists when the individual's abilities are greater than and subsume the requirements of the system. In modern society ... the structure of the social systems has changed in such a way that satisfactory competence is impossible. The diversity of ... interaction systems forces many ... to negotiate new patterns of interaction and new conceptions of their relationship that are unlike either person's ... origin.[2]

Since there is no list of strategies that will be effective across all situations, the generic approach to social skills introduced in the last chapter seems particularly applicable internationally. We need to learn what will work best for *us* in establishing, maintaining, and dissolving our relationships overseas.

Associated with this approach are somewhat different concerns for each stage of the relationship. Since there are relatively few institutionalized channels for *establishing* relationships internationally, to do so often requires a great deal of *self-*

2. Cronen, V. E., & Shuter, R. (1983). Forming intercultural bonds. In W. B. Gudykunst (Ed.), *Intercultural communications theory: Current perspectives.* Beverly Hills, CA: Sage, pp. 106–107.

*confidence* and *putting oneself in the right place at the right time.* The latter may be based more on clever planning than the spontaneity the expression seems to imply. Since rules for *maintaining* relationships are often so different and unexpected, to do so often requires a great deal of *mutual trust* and *giving the benefit of the doubt.* The latter often at times of stress when we are least inclined. And because even the definition of relationships and expectations for their duration differ so greatly internationally, we must recognize that *dissolving* them may or may not alter *future obligations* assumed by the relationship. In American culture, for instance, relationships and the obligations they entail may come and go. In many other cultures relationships are forever, or dissolving them may *not* dissolve an obligation!

## COMMUNICATION SKILLS

There is nothing blamed so often these days as *communication* for problems in contexts ranging from marriage to diplomacy. And **communication skills** are so often presented as a panacea. Yet "communication," itself, is a diversely and often vaguely defined phenomenon. And, as we have seen, differences in perceptions may be a bigger source of problems than how those perceptions are communicated. In fact, many relationships are held together by poor communication: if the participants communicated better, they would see just how different they were! Nevertheless, communication is very important: managers spend 90 percent of their time communicating, yet few ever receive any training in it—at home or abroad!

### Information Exchange and Social Influence

**Information exchange** is what many equate with "communication." It involves the exchange of messages with shared meaning that convey information necessary or useful in completing tasks in an organization. Terms like "profit," "loss," "other paid-in capital," "asset," "liability," "accounts receivable," or "miscellaneous expenses," for example, must mean about the same thing to task participants in an accounting department, and the meaning must reduce uncertainty about how to respond appropriately in the task: make a decision, state a judgment, or carry out some action. Such an exchange is usually vital to doing business anywhere, including abroad.

In exchanging information effectively participants must be concerned with *attention* and the "traditional" communication skills such as *speaking, listening,* and *feedback.* The object is to assure that the messages are *transported* from source to receiver with as little distortion as possible.

**Social influence** (or persuasion) is also often equated with "communication." It involves attempting to *change* the perceptions of another person or group so they will behave in some desired way. Like information exchange, it is an essential part of doing business anywhere: influencing a decision or an action; persuading a subordinate, partner, or client. In our influence attempts we can use reward, coercion, our legitimate authority, our expertise, control over the availability of information, or the desire of others to emulate us.[3] In all cases, however, the attempt involves using messages, and those messages must have shared meaning for them to have a predictable effect.

If we're trying to persuade a potential overseas partner to come in with us on a project and we base our appeal on the likelihood of a big, short-term profit (which to us is the reason for the deal) and he puts no value in it (desiring instead consistent, long-term gains), the persuasiveness of our message will be weak. Again, as with information exchange, if we are going to be effective persuading others, we need to know the perspective from which *they* are viewing the message used to persuade them. A key difference from information exchange, however, is that we may *not* want them to know *ours!* That is the "dark side" of influence.

But we are faced with a major problem when attempting to exchange information or influence others internationally. Whenever we communicate with others, we use *symbols.* If we wished to communicate "chair" to someone, we could (and occasionally might) hold up a real chair. In that case, everyone would understand exactly what we were trying to say. They would perceive the same chair. The meaning would be the same for them as it

---

3. Raven, B. H. (1965). Social influence and power. In I. D. Steiner & M. Fishbein (Eds.), *Current studies in social psychology.* New York: Holt, Rinehart and Winston.

is for us. But it is awkward going around holding up chairs. Other concepts like "quarterly report," "treaty," "deadline," "contract," "agreement," "responsibility," "love," and so forth are much more difficult to hold up. So when we communicate, our messages are comprised of *verbal* and *nonverbal* symbols instead.

Usually we assume that these symbols mean the same to others as they do to us, and our attempts at both information exchange and social influence are based on this assumption. But because of our different experiences with symbols, *everyone* will have a somewhat different perception of what is meant by them. A given symbol will *never* mean the same thing to anybody! Now if we say "chair"—even though everyone will perceive that symbol somewhat differently (have a different kind of chair in mind)— we will usually get something to sit on, at least if we speak the same language. But the symbols "deadline" or "incomplete report" or "contracted responsibility" or "obligation" or "unsatisfactory productivity" are much more problematic even if we are from the same organization: differences in their meaning can, and often do, get in the way of doing business effectively. Nevertheless, at home we can often get away with the improper assumption that others understand exactly what we mean. When we are trying to do business *internationally*, there is a serious likelihood that what others think we mean is insufficiently close to what we really mean to get the task done. In international situations, we almost never can get away with that assumption!

This recognition is vital to a sense of presence. It is a source of the perceived need to develop IMCs and necessary in the development process, itself. There are a number of *communication strategies*, the skills for which are critical to doing business internationally. They are usually necessary *prior to* proceeding with information exchange or social influence and are presented next.

### Matching Language

The need for participants to speak the same language is probably the most obvious aspect of international business. Everyone is aware of the importance of **matching language**, although many are surprised by how much can get done without it! Because of that awareness, an elaborated discussion here is unnecessary. We should note, however, that language matching can either occur directly (both participants speak the same language) or indirectly (through the use of an interpreter).

In the former case we must be aware that while the same language may be spoken by both participants, often the language is not the primary language of both (sometimes neither). The person for whom the language is not primary must expend much more effort speaking and listening and as a consequence will tend to tire and lose concentration more quickly, interpret meanings ideosyncratically, lose the train of reasoning, and so forth. For most of us a day-long planning meeting at home in our own language leaves us tired by the time we drive home. We should be able to empathize with the frustration and fatigue experienced by those in such sessions when the language is *not* their own: when their language is Cantonese and they're speaking English to accommodate us and every phrase requires extra concentration.

This awareness must be part of our sense of presence. As we have seen, it suggests that an IMC in these situations must stress the value of speaking slowly, having more breaks, and getting more feedback. Further, we rarely tend to attribute problems to language ("They speak the language, don't they?"). We more often attribute them to some inadequacy: our host's lack of intelligence, education, experience, manners, or social skills. Awareness of that tendency, too, must be part of our sense of presence. To the degree that we must make such evaluative judgments, we should not rely on verbal fluency to do so.

On the other hand, when using an interpreter, we must be aware that languages can rarely be translated *directly* and meaning is always mediated by that interpreter. The interpreter's own perspective must be taken into account. Often, two or more interpreters are involved, and the situation can be quite complex. Interpreters are not "translators." They are in the key role of interpreting for us the perspective and the information conveyed by the other. Thus we should place as much emphasis on becoming acquainted with the interpreter as with the hosts with whom we are doing business.

### Matching Ritual

*Ritualistic* communication occurs when the intended meaning of a message lies less in the meaning of the symbols than simply whether the culturally proper symbols are exchanged or not: meaning lies in the presence or absence of the symbols, not in the actions, emotions, or attitudes to which those symbols refer.

Thus when we say "good morning" to a colleague, the comment should *not* be understood to mean that we think it is a good morning or even that we wish him or her to have a good morning. It means that we know what is appropriate for a person like us to say to a person like them in a situation like this. We know what is appropriate in our role. We show we are competent in our culture.

On international assignments, the chief importance of **matching ritual** is as a *cultural test*: even if we speak the same language, are we and our hosts from the same organizational or national culture? If we exchange ritual smoothly—if they ask if we would like some coffee and we smoothly reply "Yes, black"— that indicates that we are most likely from at least the same organizational culture, and we can proceed with sharing information confident that the symbols exchanged have similar meaning to all. If the exchange of ritual goes less smoothly—we reply "No, I'd rather have tea with clover honey"—that indicates that we may not be from the same culture, and the sharing of information is unlikely to go smoothly either: we must *first* share with one another the perspectives from which we are interpreting meaning.

The skill to match ritual, and the attributions of cultural competence associated with it, can affect even the *motivation* to do business. The presumption is often that, if we don't demonstrate that we know expectations associated with ritual, we may not know other more important role expectations either—expectations about responsibilities, obligations, and so forth essential for doing business. If we don't demonstrate cultural competence, then we are not easily trusted and perhaps are simply viewed as unpleasant to do business with.

### Perspective Sharing

**Perspective sharing** involves exchanging with one another the perspective from which we are approaching a task and from which we are attributing meaning to events and symbols. It is particularly important when participants are coming from different cultures because this meaning might be quite different. If we're reviewing the accounts of an overseas subsidiary, we must first determine if we and our hosts are making judgments from the perspective of the same accounting system or, in fact, are coming from different systems with somewhat different usages of terms—"profit," "loss," "asset" again for example—and bases for making judgments.

Perspective sharing leads to an *awareness* of the perspective of the other persons. At a minimum, such an awareness is a necessary prerequisite to both exchanging information and persuasion. On an international assignment without an understanding of the perspective from which our host is giving and receiving information, that "information" is at best meaningless, at worst misleading. As Cronan and Shuter state, "the development of a third culture demands that intercultural communicators establish common communicative ground—how individuals accomplish this certainly warrants close attention."[4]

Hall differentiates between low- and high-context communication.[5] In **low-context communication** the burden of information exchange lies in the symbols themselves (the words) such that if anything very complex must be communicated, it takes lots of words often arranged complexly. Reporting to our boss on the success of our recent assignment would in this case involve an elaborated description of assignment objectives, what we did to meet those objectives, difficulties we had along the way, and the outcome. It would be a rather long affair whether oral or written. **High-context communication** on the other hand relies heavily on the context of the interaction (including the participants' shared experience and their relationship to one another) to convey information: the symbols only serve as "cues" to the salient aspects of the context. In high-context communication the meaning of the symbols cannot be fully understood without reference to that context. Making the report in this case might consist solely of a wide smile and "great!" We know our boss is aware of the objectives, that he has been on such assignments, himself, and can guess much of what we did and our difficulties. Our smile both makes all that salient and communicates the outcome.

Cultures differ significantly in the extent to which they use generally high- versus low-context communication:

> In a low-context culture, like that of the United States, where very little is taken for granted, greater cultural diversity and

---

4. Cronen et al. Forming intercultural bonds. p. 98.

5. Hall, E. T. (1981). *Beyond culture*. Garden City, NY: Anchor Press.

heterogeneity are likely to make verbal skills more necessary and, therefore, more highly prized. One of the qualifications of a group leader, indeed, is his or her ability of verbal expression. . . . In a high-context culture, such as Japan's, however, cultural homogeneity encourages suspicion of verbal skills, confidence in the unspoken, and eagerness to avoid confrontation. The Japanese have even developed *haragei*, or the "art of the belly," for the meeting of minds or at least the viscera, without clear verbal interaction. Verbal ability is not necessarily required of Japanese leaders.[6]

Communication problems occur on international assignments when going *from* a country with a high-context language *to* one with a low-context language in that we become overwhelmed with words while trying to ascertain what the words are cueing or how they are related to the context: the people seem to be "all words and no substance!" Problems also occur when we go *from* a low-context language *to* a high-context one in that we are looking for words and get far too few of them to make any sense of things. Often what is said at different times and in different contexts seems contradictory: the people seem "inscrutable!" In both transitions there is a need to *match the level of context* between participants.

Further, as people communicate with one another to complete tasks within organizations, they develop higher- and higher-context communication. They share more and more experience, and the *elaboration* of messages becomes less necessary. Different organizations develop different high-context languages within the same industry simply as a function of convergence of an organization's personnel with one another and divergence from personnel in other organizations. Even different departments within the same organization or different work teams within the same department commonly develop somewhat different high-context languages. This is certainly true of different offices of a multinational or global company or differences between the "home office" and an international "branch office." Much of the difficulty of interorganizational and interdepartmental com-

---

6. Okabe, R. (1983). Cultural assumptions of east and west: Japan and the United States. In W. B. Gudykunst (Ed.), *Intercultural communications theory: Current perspectives*. Beverly Hills, CA: Sage, pp. 38–39.

munication stems from differences in high-context languages. Because these languages often use the same words, we *think* we understand what the other is saying: it's only much later when the contract falls through, the treaty is violated, or the report is not submitted on time that we realize that the meanings were different! In such situations there is a need to *match high-context meaning*.

In international business, there is rarely much common experience, and so there is usually a need for all participants to *lower their level of context* to share information effectively. IMCs, for example, should typically rely more on verbal communication to confer meaning because it is generally of lower context than nonverbal communication. There is evidence, in fact, that managers of cross-cultural programs commonly use *a low profile but verbal style.*[7]

### Matching Agendas

We have all watched little children playing alongside each other and *apparently* talking with one another. If we listen closely to the dialogue, however, it is commonly something like the following:

**René:** "I can't find my red block."
**Lori:** "My mother is late again."
**René:** "I thought I put it here but it's gone."
**Lori:** "She was late yesterday, too."
**René:** "If I don't find it by 5 o'clock I'm going to scream!"
**Lori:** "If mother isn't here by 5 o'clock I'm going to cry!"

And at 5 o'clock René screams and Lori cries and it would seem that they had discussed it and arranged to have a riot. What the children had learned was that it's much easier to talk if they take turns. What they hadn't yet learned was that they need to talk about the *same topic* at the *same time*!

---

7. Mumford, S. J. (1983). The cross-cultural experience: The program manager's perspective. In D. Landis & R. W. Brislin (Eds.), *Handbook of intercultural training.* Vol. II: *Issues in training methodology.* New York: Pergamon.

As adults in organizations we are usually better at **matching agendas**. Or at least better at appearing to! But not always:

**Manager:** "How's your monthly report coming?"

**Supervisor:** "I'm having trouble with Ram."

**Manager:** "I need it next week or the CEO will be on my back."

**Supervisor:** "I think I'll transfer him to Yadav's unit."

**Manager:** "What?"

**Supervisor:** "I think I'll transfer him to Yadav's unit."

**Manager:** "What about your report? All the others are ready to go!"

In any meeting each participant has several agenda items he or she wishes to be dealt with. Those items are usually prioritized in some way. But the overlap of items and priorities is rarely perfect—or even good. What frequently happens is that they talk to us about their first agenda item while we "fade off." When they've finished we talk to them about our first agenda item while they "fade off" (and we know they do because we know we do it). Without matching agendas, meetings typically end with all participants happy because they all said what they wanted to say, but the meetings are otherwise failures because no information is exchanged.

Without matched agendas, there is no opportunity to *share* information—or anything else. Nothing is being shared but *time*. Internationally, because of likely differences in agenda items or at least their priorities, a much more prepared and explicit agenda may be required. Discussion of the agenda, itself, can be an important aspect of doing business abroad as we frequently see in diplomatic negotiations. In such cases agenda *formulating, matching,* and *monitoring* are important components of an IMC.

The point of matching language, matching ritual, perspective sharing, and matching agendas is to allow us to converge adequately on the meaning of symbols so that they do, in fact, convey information: they do reduce uncertainty. All too frequently, in our rush to "get down to business" or "get to the point," we exchange messages with symbols that have insufficiently shared meaning, the exchange is unproductive, and the business is not done well. A little "let's have some tea first" or "let's first get to know one another a bit" or "what's on your mind?" is essential.

## Presence in Telecommunication

Thus far reference to a sense of presence has been in the context of face-to-face interaction. As noted in Chapter 1 most international business is done in that context: we must literally "go international." However, with the interface of new telecommunication and computer technologies more and more international business is being done through telemediated channels. No longer are mediated encounters restricted in time and richness as in a letter or telex. The new technologies allow for the rapid exchange of messages along both audio and video channels. The increasing availability, cost-effectiveness, and simple appeal of teleconferencing and videoconferencing promise to increase their role in international business. The inevitability of their use requires us all to develop the skills to use them effectively.

There are, however, some important implications of this new technology for communication skills. Currently the new technologies are heavily *information oriented.* In fact, they are sometimes called "the new information technologies." Their efficiency in communicating *information* is, in part, their appeal. They can provide a major new dimension to symbol *transportation* across distances. But are the symbols transported really "information" in terms of their having shared meaning? We have seen that information exchange must be based on a foundation of a common perspective. Within our own culture, that assumption is (usually) acceptably valid. In international communication, it certainly is not.

Without an adequately shared perspective, the "information" conveyed so rapidly by telecommunication media has the potential for ambiguity, confusion, *mis*communication, and mistakes. Determination of cost-effectiveness must take into account the high costs of those mistakes. For the new technologies to be useful internationally—to be truly cost-effective—we need to develop the skill with them to share perspectives as well as information. We need the skill to match rituals to provide a "test" for the necessity of that perspective sharing and match agendas to assure that we are communicating *with*, not simply talking *to*, those at the other end. And we have to develop IMCs sensitive to the ecological characteristics of these technologies.

Effective use of telecommunication technology will necessitate a better understanding of the requirements of developing a **sense of** *remote* **presence.** Lessons may be learned from research in the U.S. Navy on the development of remote presence in "teleoperators." This research involves assessing the impact of maximized sensory channels on the operation of undersea vehicles by surface operators. In telemediated international communication we also need to be aware of the remote ecology of our hosts, as well as the characteristics of the medium we are using, to do business effectively.

Different media vary in what is called **social presence**: the "degree of salience of the other person in the interaction and the consequent salience of the interpersonal relationships."[8] Unlike a sense of presence, it is a characteristic of the communication medium. Media have social presence to the degree that they facilitate participant awareness of the social component of their ecology. Generally, media high in social presence are those that convey more nonverbal symbols. Typically video, multichannel audio, telephone, monaural audio, speakerphone, and written media are found to have social presence decreasing in that order.

We need to select a medium with the level of social presence required for the task. For some tasks the audio mode of teleconferencing might be adequate; for others (requiring visual displays or better appreciation of emotional issues) videoconferencing might be the only acceptable substitute for face-to-face exchange. Certainly awareness of a medium's social presence is part of the sense of presence needed to develop an IMC in mediated contexts.

## STRESS-MANAGEMENT SKILLS

**Stress** is the body's reaction to demands placed on it by the environment.[9-11] These demands are commonly called **stressors**. Stress is a necessary part of living. Without reacting to the

---

8. Short, J., Williams, E., & Christie, B. (1976). *The social psychology of telecommunications.* New York: John Wiley, p. 65.

9. Meichenbaum, D. (1977). *Cognitive-behavior modification: An integrative approach.* New York: Plenum.

10. Smith, R. E. (1980). Development of an integrative coping response through cognitive-affective stress management training. In I. G. Sarason & C. D. Spielberger (Eds.), *Stress and anxiety*, Vol. 7. New York: John Wiley.

11. Sarason, I. G., Sarason, B. R., & Johnson, J. H. (1980). *Stressful life events: Measurement, moderators, and adaptation.* Technical Report for the Office of Naval Research, CO 001, Arlington, VA.

stressors of life, we die. In fact clinical definitions of death are associated with the body's failure to respond to specific stressors. Stress is not good or bad: it is simply necessary. This is a key point to understand if stress generally, and ecoshock in particular, is to be effectively managed.

If stress is managed *well*, it can have positive effects. An optimal level of stress is necessary for proper functioning in many tasks. It is particularly critical when people must perform near their maximum potential: the athlete, the actor, the race car driver, the executive. These people know that stress is necessary, and they must learn to use it positively or their performances will be inadequate. If stress is managed *poorly*, it has largely negative effects. Too much stress (or too little) interferes with performance.

Stress is a complex physiological response called the **general adaptation syndrome (GAS)** involving the central and peripheral nervous systems, and the cardiovascular and endocrine systems.[12] It prepares the body to deal with a stressor and generally involves an initial **alarm stage** with the production of adrenaline and a subsequent orientation response; a **resistance stage** in which the body is actively attempting to cope with the stressor; and, sometimes, an **exhaustion stage** in which the body's resources are depleted.[13]

The GAS is rarely perfect, however. Imbalances in system reactions can produce an ineffective response to the stressor: perceptual-motor coordination and cognitive ability may be hampered. For instance, there is good evidence that high stress is dysfunctional in negotiation, leading to hostility and simplistic perceptual, cognitive, and group structuring.[14] We cannot be close to 100 percent *present* if stress levels are *too high* and, as a consequence, our perceptual focus is *too narrow*. We can, in fact, become distracted by the physiological symptoms of stress themselves—our increased heartbeat, muscle tension, flushing, or sweating. With too much stress, we simply cannot attain a sense of people, place, time, task, or other critical characteristics of the

---

12. Selye, H. (1956). *The stress of life.* New York: McGraw-Hill.

13. Barna, L. M. (1983). The stress factor in intercultural relations. In D. Landis & R. W. Brislin (Eds.), *Handbook of intercultural training,*Vol. II: *Issues in training methodology.* New York: Pergamon.

14. Hopmann, P. T., & Walcott. (1977). In D. Druckman (Ed.), *Negotiations: Social-psychological perspectives.* Beverly Hills, CA: Sage.

task ecology. Likewise, if our stress level is *too low*, we are insufficiently alert to these characteristics and alternative responses to them. We must have the skill to monitor adequately our stress levels, determine the level at which we function best, and manage stress to maintain that optimal level.

Prolonged stress can produce wearing effects on the body leading to migrain, hypertension, heart disease, hyperthyroidism, diarrhea, constipation, peptic ulcers, sleeplessness, shortness of breath, exhaustion, fatigue, and lingering illnesses. Sustained high levels of adrenaline appear to inhibit the body's immune system—we "catch" everything that's around. The long-term effects of stress can involve psychological problems, increased accidents, and breakdowns in social skills—the same symptoms discussed with ecoshock in Chapter 4. The mate of stress is illness, whether the stressor is perceived positively or negatively. The irony is, of course, that the very reaction essential to our effectiveness and, ultimately, survival can also eventually be the cause of our demise—particularly in high-stress occupations.

On international assignments we must, of course, cope not only with the stressors normally associated with doing whatever kind of business we do, but we must also cope with ecoshock. We must cope with both in a context in which our habitual coping strategies may not be effective. And we frequently must do this without the organizational and social support that normally play a large role in helping to maintain appropriate levels of stress at home.[15]

There are lots of strategies people typically use to cope with stress, and an important part of stress-management is selecting one that fits the ecology in which we find ourselves. For instance, we can:

| | |
|---|---|
| Escape the stressor | Confront it |
| Sleep | Drink |
| Eat | Take drugs |
| Take it out on others | Pray |
| Make love | Work |
| Exercise | Watch sports |
| Meditate | Share it |

15. Fontaine, G. (1986). Roles of social support systems in overseas relocation. *International Journal of Intercultural Relations, 10,* 361–378.

| | |
|---|---|
| Attempt suicide | Cry |
| Sightsee | Accept it |
| Run from it | Analyze it |
| Wait for it to go away | Put it in perspective |
| Shop | Get sick |
| Get help | Relax |
| Ignore it | Smoke |
| Feel sorry for ourselves | Go for a drive |
| Find a hobby | Get angry |
| Seek solitude | Socialize |

We could *all* add to this list. It represents the *tools* we use for coping with stress. On international assignments we typically have no new or different ones from which to choose. We may have *fewer* because of the unavailability or inappropriateness of some. Note that none of these tools are necessarily good or bad—we can kill ourselves confronting an unsolvable problem, be hopelessly incapacitated by trying to analyze something too complex, or get through it all by taking a drink and relaxing. It all depends on who we are, the nature of the stressor, and the *skills* we have. All the tools require skills to use them effectively: working, drinking, eating, shopping, meditating. Without the skills, they will all fail or, worse, exacerbate the stress.

Each of us must—if we haven't already—identify our own "tool kit." Are we a running-shopping-angry person? Or a drinking-confronting-sports person? Or a meditating-relaxing-running person? Or whatever? A first step in learning to cope better is to know how we cope now! Identification of our own tools is important because they are what keep us alive, happy, and successful—or not. Because stress is so pervasive in our lives, much of what we are as a person, our personality, is described by the tools we use to cope with stress.

Although our tool kit may be rather sparce, *prior* to a crisis most of us aren't too worried because we assume that "when the pressure is on, we'll be up to the task": that is, *in* the crisis we'll be able to bring out new ways to cope, to do what we have to do even if we've never done it before. Unfortunately, most evidence indicates that the more critical the crisis, the more we rely on our habitual coping strategies. Most of us don't have special tools for crises. Yet doing business internationally can involve continual, unexpected crises. If our habitual tools don't work (and often they don't!), we do worse, not better, in these situations.

Again, we must look at our own tool kit. It usually works in our own ecology, matched to who we are, what our resources are, and the stressors we typically confront. But will it be adequate for different stressors in a different world—for coping effectively with ecoshock? One characteristic of a successful diplomat, businessperson, or advisor is having a *broader range of coping strategies available*: a bigger selection of tools from which to choose when the international assignment necessitates it!

## A FINAL NOTE

We have now taken a look at the skill package personnel on international assignments most need to develop IMCs and do business effectively. It includes a sense of presence and social, communication, and stress-management skills. They are summarized in Figure 7.1. I turn now and for the remainder of this book to how organizations can best manage international assignments so that their personnel have these skills.

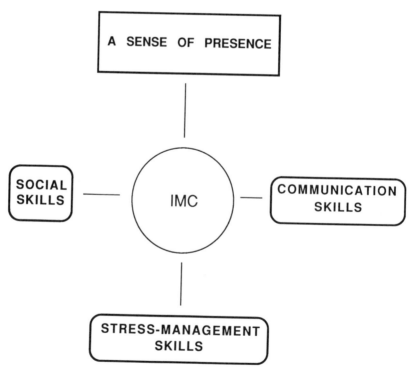

**Figure 7.1**    Skills for Developing IMCs

# SCREENING, SELF-SELECTION, AND ORIENTATION

Chapter 8

Up to this point we have examined the ecology of international assignments, the dual challenge of coping with ecoshock and doing business within that ecology, commonly described strategies for doing that business, the key IMC strategy needed to do it consistently effectively, and the skills *we as personnel* require to develop IMCs. I rotate the perspective a bit in this and the next two chapters and examine what *our organization* must do to best assure that we on assignment have those skills. The focus is on the **organizational strategy** most effective in assisting personnel on assignments and the roles in it of the **programs** through which assistance can be provided: screening, self-selection, orientation, training, arranging travel and accommodation, and organizational and social support.

## MANAGEMENT, NOT JUST *TRAINING*

Commonly organizations provide only a few of the programs that could potentially assist those on international assignments. They may, for instance, provide language training, previsits to the overseas site, information about their international operations, or just "survival tips." The decision on what to provide is usually based more on resource priorities, requests from overseas personnel, or some manager's hunch than a well-thought-out strategy.

While training or any of the other organizational programs can individually be useful in assisting assignment effectiveness, accumulated international experience suggests that more sophisticated strategies involving coordinated programs are necessary. We don't know how to train well enough, and maybe *can* never know how, for training alone ever to be sufficient preparation for assignments. The same can be said for screening, orientation, and so forth. Doing business internationally is not something that can just be trained for—it must be *managed*.

*That is the THIRD THEME of this book.*

Management involves focusing all organizational programs on providing personnel with the skills required for successful international assignments.

## THE OBJECTIVES FOR MANAGING INTERNATIONAL ASSIGNMENTS

In examining how organizations can best manage their international assignments, we face many of the same issues confronted in doing business on our own particular assignment. Much of the difficulty in specifying the best organizational strategy has been the ambiguity (or at least inconsistency) in identifying the *objectives* of such a strategy. That is, what are screening, training, support, and other programs supposed to provide that will help personnel do their assignments better? Again, much of that ambiguity stems from lack of theoretical clarity about *what it means to be effective* and *what skills personnel need* to be so.

Sometimes assignment effectiveness is seen in task completion terms: "Getting the job done well, period." But often it is seen as involving adjustment, satisfaction, culture learning, personal growth, forming relationships with clients, making good impressions on hosts, being liked, not causing incidents, and so forth. As a consequence, although researchers have specified a variety of "skills," "traits," or "competencies" that can be determinants of effectiveness, the lists vary considerably. The provision of any or all of them could be seen as *potential* objectives for managing international assignments. Table 8.1 presents a list of those more commonly specified.

According to Kealey and Rubin, the ideal profile of someone on an international assignment would be

an individual who is truly *open to* and *interested in* other people and their ideas, capable of building relationships of trust among people. *He or she is sensitive to the feelings and thoughts of another*, expresses *respect* and positive regard for others, and is *nonjudgmental*. Finally, he or she tends to be *self-confident*, is able to take *initiative*, is *calm* in situations of frustration [or] ambiguity, and is *not rigid*. The individual is also a *technically* or *professionally competent* person.[1]

The ideal composite profile of such skills has been variously labeled as "overseasmanship"[2] or "multicultural man" [sic].[3] But again, I must emphasize that most of the research on skills or traits predictive of success is not based on clearly defined criteria of effectiveness. As Kealey and Rubin warn, despite the common descriptions of an "overseas type,"

> the *limited usefulness* of such a type needs to be emphasized. . . . [It] is an abstraction, an ideal; no individual fits the type perfectly and indeed our generalization does not at all imply the notion of "the highest amount of empathy, etc. as being the ideal. The generalization goes only so far as to suggest that a certain amount of these capabilities is desirable. *The emphasis given to any specific trait will depend on the nature of the task to be accomplished and the environmental conditions that will affect adjustment and effectiveness.*[4]

Further, Benson stresses that

> Overseas adjustment can vary so much from region to region, country to country that what is needed is to match specific individuals and environments rather than determine global criteria for the measurement of an individual's probable adaptability without reference to a specific culture. All of these issues would question the notion that overseas adjustment is "a" thing or process. Rather, it may be necessary to look at specific cross-cultural situations and determine criterion

---

1. From D. J. Kealey & B. D. Ruben, Cross-cultural personnel selection criteria, issues, and methods, in D. Landis & R. W. Brislin (Eds.), *Handbook of intercultural training.* Vol. 1: *Issues in theory and design.* New York: Pergamon Press, 1983. Reprinted with permission.

2. Cleveland, H., Mangone, G. J., & Adams, J. C. (1960). *The overseas Americans.* New York: McGraw-Hill.

3. Adler, P. S. (1977). Beyond cultural identity: Reflections on cultural and multicultural man. In R. W. Brislin (Ed.), *Culture learning: Concepts, applications, and research.* Honolulu: University of Hawaii Press.

4. Kealey & Ruben. Cross-cultural personnel selection criteria, p. 166.

**TABLE 8.1**   List of skills, traits, or competencies commonly thought to be associated with international effectiveness

| | |
|---|---|
| Empathy | Courtesy |
| Flexibility | Adaptability |
| Patience | Tolerance for ambiguity |
| Openness | Perseverance |
| Reliability | Integrity |
| Confidence | Language skills |
| Emotional stability | Ability to manage stress |
| Communication skills | Social skills |
| Tolerance for differences | Ability to respond quickly |
| Humor | Ability to accept failure |
| Resourcefulness | Self-relience |
| Sensitivity | Realism |
| Teaching skills | Team skills |
| Ability to handle alcohol | Sincerity |
| Curiosity | Interest in host culture |
| Positive regard for others | Technical knowledge |
| Acceptability of assignment | Nonjudmentalness |
| Reliability | Positive self-image |
| Desire to go abroad | Quickness in responding |
| Initiative | Honesty |
| Nonethnocentrism | Political sensitivity |
| High motivation | Managerial ability |

Previous overseas experience
Desire to collect experiences
Potential for growth in company
Physical attributes such as health, gender, or appearance
All of the above in the spouse and children

dimensions relevant to them, such that there are as many kinds of overseas adaptation as there are cross-cultural situations.[5]

Thus there has been ample difficulty for organizations in specifying the objectives of their *programs* or *strategy* for managing international assignments. As stated in Chapter 1, the goal of this book is to provide both practical and conceptual clarity with respect to these objectives. To this end I must reiterate the point developed earlier that on an international assignment, per-

5. Benson, P. G. (1978). Measuring cross-cultural adjustment: The problem of criteria. *International Journal of Intercultural Relations, 2*, 21–37.

sonnel require the skills to face *two* major challenges: (1) coping with ecoshock and (2) developing a strategy to do business effectively in a different ecology. Assisting personnel on each of these must be the *dual* objectives of organizations for managing international assignments.

## A *MANAGEMENT* STRATEGY

A **management strategy** is generally viewed as involving (1) development of objectives and policies; (2) appraisal of resources; (3) planning programs necessary to meet objectives and assessing their likely impact; (4) organizing, coordinating, and integrating the implementation of those programs; and (5) evaluating the success of the programs in meeting objectives. All these steps are necessary for properly managing international assignments as well: What are the objectives? What resources are available? What programs are needed to meet the objectives? How should those programs be coordinated? How will we know if the strategy has been successful?

In managing international assignments, particular concern should be with planning, organizing, coordinating, integrating, and evaluating the following programs:

- *Screening* and *self-selection* for assignments based on criteria of demonstrated usefulness in predicting effectiveness in the assigned ecologies.
- *Orienting* personnel to the assigned ecologies in terms of information useful to being effective in them.
- *Training* personnel in the technical, professional, language, and intercultural skills necessary to do business with their hosts in those ecologies.
- *Arranging* for *travel* and *accommodation* to lessen their negative impact on effectiveness and facilitate IMC development.
- *Providing* for full *organizational* and *social support* for assigned personnel and dependents with a particular concern on buffering ecoshock and facilitating IMC development.

Thus in a strategy for managing international assignments, we must select candidates who either already can use a sense of presence and have adequate social, communication, and stress-management skills or have the potential to acquire them readily. We must provide them with the information and training they need to make best use of or to improve their skills. We must assist them in properly arranging travel and accommodation. And we must provide the social and organizational support necessary to nurture them while they are there. None of these are independent of the others. They must be planned, organized, and so forth: they must be *managed*.

There is an interesting comparison between the strategy required by *personnel* to do business successfully on individual assignments and that required by their *organizations* in managing many such assignments. This comparison is depicted in Figure 8.1. For the former, I have proposed that the most effective

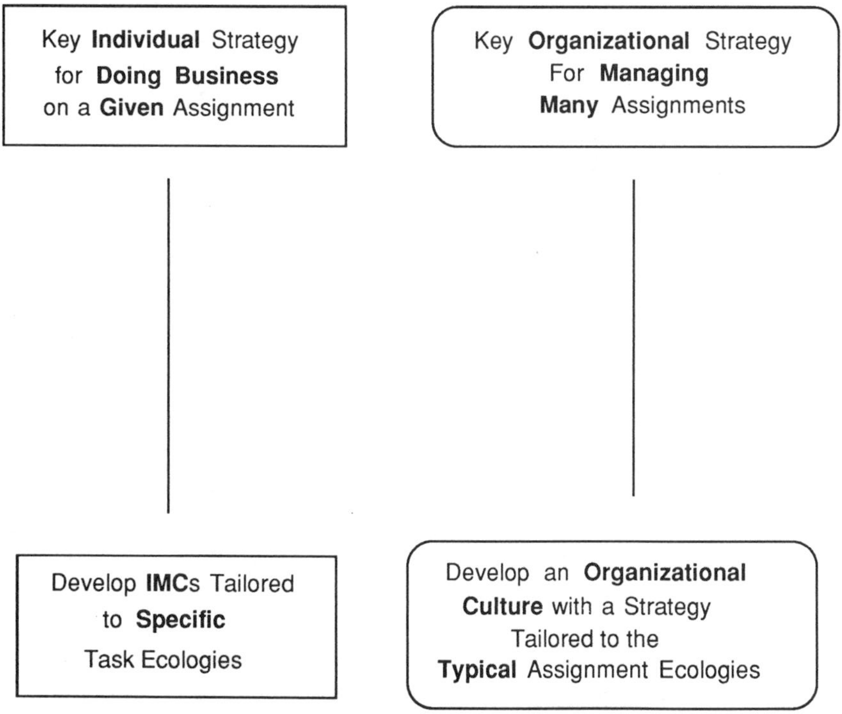

Key **Individual** Strategy
for **Doing Business**
on a **Given** Assignment

Key **Organizational** Strategy
For **Managing**
**Many** Assignments

Develop **IMCs** Tailored
to **Specific**
Task Ecologies

Develop an **Organizational**
**Culture** with a Strategy
Tailored to the
**Typical** Assignment Ecologies

**Figure 8.1**  Individual and Organizational Strategies for Successful International Assignments

strategy is the development of IMCs tailored to the task ecologies associated with their assignment. But the point has been made that these task ecologies are rarely fully knowable by the organization prior to the assignment. So for the organization, I propose that the most effective strategy is the development of organizational cultures tailored to the international assignment ecologies at the organizational level most commonly faced by their personnel. Because these ecologies will often have important *similarities* for a particular organization, it is useful to develop generalized procedures for managing them.

## A *GENERIC* STRATEGY

Because international assignment ecologies at the organizational level can vary considerably from one type of organization to another (diplomatic versus commercial, for instance), it is impossible to describe a specific strategy for managing assignments that is best for all organizations. Again, there is no rule of thumb or step-by-step recipe. As just indicated, however, international assignments for a *particular* organization often *do* have a degree of ecological consistency, thus the legitimacy for that organization to develop a strategy of managing assignments as part of its organizational culture. Because of this consistency, it is also feasible to learn what specific strategy works best for that organization through some form of iterative feedback process. Thus for a given organization, there is both the *need* and the *opportunity* to use a **generic strategy** for managing international assignments: a strategy for selecting the specific strategy most tailored to the organization's requirements and resources.

A generic strategy provides the necessary flexibility for organizations to "learn how to learn" how to best manage *their* international assignments to meet the objectives of assisting personnel in coping with ecoshock and doing business. The strategy involves:

1. Assessing the international ecologies most commonly faced by organizational personnel on assignment in terms of those characteristics that set them apart from domestic assignments and that differentiate them one from another. It must involve defining specifically the *criteria of success*

on assignments. It should involve identifying tasks which typically must be completed, describing the ecological characteristics likely to be important in them, and assessing the skills *necessary* and those *possessed* by available personnel to develop IMCs appropriate to those ecologies.

This *task analysis* is like an "awareness of the necessary" at the organizational level. It is, however, much more analytical and less immediate and intuitive than that at the personal level. Rather, the concern is more with developing something of a stereotype of ecological characteristics most commonly faced by organizational personnel on their assignments.

2. Identifying a range of specific, alternative strategies for meeting the dual objectives of managing international asssignments through programs for screening, self-selection, orientation, training, arranging travel and accommodation, and support. It involves expanding the organization's perceptions of appropriate strategies beyond those commonly used for assisting personnel on domestic assignments. This is like an "awareness of the possible" at the organizational level. The key is to remember that the range of strategies commonly employed domestically will likely be too narrow to meet the more complex requirements of managing international assignments.

3. Selecting a specific strategy that specifies programs and a way of coordinating and integrating them likely to best meet the requirements given the typical assignment ecologies and the organization's personnel and resources. The strategy selected that is best for one organization may not be the best for another. That is the key to the generic approach: Selecting a strategy responsive to our organization's requirements, not somebody else's.

This selection is like an "awareness of the desirable" at the organizational level. Again, however, it is much more analytical and less immediate and intuitive than at the personal level.

4. Implementing the selected strategy. The organization must do it. It mustn't select one strategy and then do something else, like fall back on its organizational "habits." It must also commit the resources necessary for success and give the

strategy time to be developed and to work! It takes years, at least, for an organization to learn how best to manage domestic assignments, often accompanied by lots of mistakes: it shouldn't expect a new strategy for international assignments to work perfectly the first time. It needs *realistic* expectations of the time and resources required and the level of performance to be expected.

5. Evaluating the success of the selected strategy in meeting the objectives across a number of assignments and personnel. Does it work? If not, why? Was the task analysis inade-

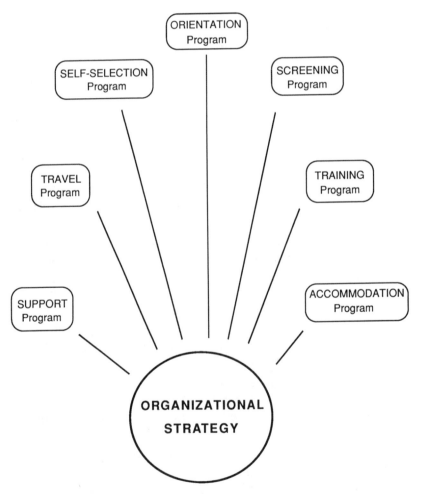

**Figure 8.2**   Strategy for Managing International Assignments

quate? Was the organization insufficiently comprehensive or innovative in specifying a range of alternative strategies? Was an inappropriate one selected? Was it implemented poorly or the necessary resources not committed? Or has there simply been insufficient time for the strategy to be developed?

This generic strategy provides a way to select an organizationally appropriate specific one for managing international assignments involving programs for screening, self-selection, orientation, and so forth as depicted in Figure 8.2. This and the next two chapters examine key issues associated with these programs. The examination is principally from the perspective of their role in facilitating the management objectives presented earlier: assisting personnel to develop skills to cope with ecoshock and do business effectively in a different ecology. The *emphasis* is on the role of each program in helping assigned personnel develop IMCs and the associated skills. The *goal* is to provide guidance to organizations in developing a strategy to use these programs most effectively.

# SCREENING

A **screening program** for international assignments involves assessing prospective candidates on physical, demographic, performance, personality, social, and organizational criteria thought to be associated with assignment effectiveness. The presumption is that, if such criteria can be identified, it is far easier to screen for candidates who meet them than it is to select candidates who don't and *change* them into those that do. It saves time, money, and trauma for all involved.

## Traditional Approaches

Reliance on screening is based on the assumption that (1) there is a broad range of prospective candidates from which to choose, (2) there are criteria of effectiveness available, and (3) there are valid procedures for assessing candidates on them. Some organizations simply don't have the range of candidates from which to choose or they may not have much control over whom they have. Other organizations may recruit principally on technical or professional criteria unrelated to the requirements of international assignments. Commonly, the organization is in the disadvantageous position of eliminating those who obviously *don't* meet the criteria from a selection list that is quite limited: screening is often more screening *out* than screening *in.*

In reviewing the screening programs of organizations doing international business, Kealey and Rubin conclude that the

> methods employed in the selection of cross-cultural personnel range from the rigorous assessment center techniques used in some organizations to the simple and straightforward solicitation of willing volunteers in other agencies. At what point along the continuum between these two extremes a particular organization's selection methodology falls depends upon a number of factors including: the size of the organization; the extent of resources allocated to the selection process; the extent of the organization's involvement in cross-cultural projects; the number of potential candidates for available positions; the amount of time available to complete the selection process; the failure rate on the given organization's previous cultural projects; and the competency and experience of the personnel staff with regard to the theory and practice in the cross-cultural domain.[6]

Commonly the home office uses the same criteria to select personnel for international assignments as they do at home: their demonstrated skill in doing business domestically. This appears to be the case despite the many important differences between the domestic and international assignments described by countless overseas personnel and in this—and several other—books. As Mumford-Fowler states;

> In both public- and private-sector organizations, people are selected for overseas assignment based on technical skills, availability, and other factors, but not on their ability to get along overseas. Even in the world of diplomacy, people are

---

6. Kealey & Ruben. Cross-cultural personnel selection criteria, p. 170.

not sent overseas because they are adaptable, empathetic, persevering, patient, courteous, or other operationally difficult-to-define qualities.[7]

### The Role in Managing International Assignments

The role of screening in managing international assignments is *to identify those potential candidates for such assignments best able to cope with ecoshock and do business in a way compatible with the assignment ecology*—those most able to develop IMCs. This involves identifying those who have and use (or could most quickly acquire) a sense of presence and associated social, communication, and stress-management skills and those most likely to be able to find and become part of IMC networks. These, then, become screening criteria tied to management objectives designed to facilitate successful international assignments.

So the **screening questions** become "Who are these people?" "Who are the people in our organization with a sense of presence? With practical intelligence?" "Who are the people good at working in novel taskes or at times of organizational transition?" "Who are good with new or culturally diverse employees and clients?" "Who are best at communicating with a variety of people from different perspectives in unstructured situations?" "Who have a large *variety* of friends and associates?" "Who can establish good working relationships and maintain them under stress?" "Who manages stress well?" "Who has a sense of presence at the times it's needed?" "Who relies on habits only when those habits are useful?" Watch. These are the candidates most likely to have what's needed for international assignments. Remember, they *may not be* the ones most effective in the relatively stable domestic ecologies, in the repetitive tasks, the one's who "fit in" so well with the organizational culture. But they *are* the people who are good at *times of change*, the *microculture* people, the *innovators*.

And "How does the organization find them?" The procedures for *assessing* these skills are much more usefully based on *actual*

---

7. Mumford, S. J. (1983). The cross-cultural experience: The program manager's perspective. In D. Landis & R. W. Brislin (Eds.), *Handbook of intercultural training.* Vol. II: *Issues in training methodology.* New York: Pergamon, p. 95.

*behavior* in applicable organizational settings than on the "paper and pencil" measures upon which assessment so typically relies. And good assessment is not a "one-time" thing: it requires careful observation of performance across a range of tasks with varied ecologies, over time, and under stress. Particular emphasis in these observations should be on candidate performance on tasks ecologically most similar to those likely to be encountered on international assignments: tasks that—while completed at home— still involve differences from other domestic assignments in place, time, travel, communication, people, support, and structure. Most commonly, these tasks will involve differences in only one or two of these characteristics, but performance on them can still be both revealing and usefully predictive of performance internationally.

For such observation to be done best, managers responsible for selection need to understand well the internationl assignment ecologies their overseas personnel typically face. They, as well as their personnel, need *orientation* to the assignment ecologies. Orientation programs are examined shortly. At this point it is only noted that orientation for these managers should consist of information about the international sites acquired from sources at the home office or, better yet, by visiting those sites themselves. Such visits are frequently made by upper-level managers. But it must be emphasized that from the perspective of assisting in the selection of future candidates, the purpose of such visits is *not* to ascertain simply how well the current personnel on assignment are performing, but *what ecologically they are faced with* and *what they are doing* that is or isn't working.

## SELF-SELECTION

The organization needs a program for screening potential candidates for an international assignment *out* or *in* based on criteria related to management objectives. But often the best "screener" is the potential candidate, himself or herself. *We* can often make the best assessment of whether we meet the criteria—have the skills—or not. *We* can often best answer the "screening questions." We know if we have and use a sense of presence in new or different situations. We know how well we handle stress, how well we communicate, how easily we form relationships with a variety of people, and so forth. We know best if our family can "take it" coming along or being left behind. We are the best judge of whether we *want* to go, our spouse wants to go, and how successful we've been overseas in the past. We and our spouse are the best judges of the likely impact on his or her career. The organization needs a **self-selection program**, too.

Self-selection is a process in which the potential candidates for assignments make a determination as to their suitability both in terms of competence and motivation. They can only make this determination to the degree that they know clearly the mission on the assignment, the tasks they are going to encounter, the ecologies of those tasks, and the skills required to complete them effectively. They need to be educated or informed. They need some orientation to the potential assignment prior to selecting to participate in it, not just after that selection. Candidates for international assignments and their organization need to work together to decide who is well suited to go international.

Thus one of the important issues associated with *managing international assignments is that screening, self-selection and orientation programs must be closely coordinated and integrated.* The organization's strategy should not just include one of them or each of them independently or in sequence. Further, in most cases, it is important that *all* relevant personnel from executives to clerks receive basic orientation to the international activities of the organization and the opportunities and requirements of international assignments. They all are *potential* candidates, and it is far better that they have years to answer for themselves the "screening questions" than a week or so!

## ORIENTATION

**Orientation programs** provide information about international assignments necessary or useful for completing them effectively. This typically includes information about the host culture and ecology and living and working in it, about the international operations of the organization, and about preparation requirements for the assignment. It sometimes includes more specific information about the tasks and people that will be encountered. As we have seen, at least some orientation is useful along with screening and self-selection prior to identification of those actually assigned.

Orientation has suffered from the same ambiguity or inconsistency in specifying criteria of assignment effectiveness as have screening and self-selection. As a consequence, there has been a lack of clarity as to just what information needs to be provided and how best to provide it. The need is to improve the clarity by relating it to objectives for managing international assignments.

### Traditional Approaches

Most typically orientation provides information about the host culture and ecology. A list of the kinds of information commonly presented includes the following:

- History
- Geography
- Literature
- Political and economic system
- Current events
- Important people such as politicians, discoverers, artists, sports stars, and actors
- Achievement in science and industry
- Religions
- Values
- Customs
- Holidays
- Languages
- Things to see and do

Often the list includes information helpful for living and working in the host culture:

- Cost of living
- Exchange rates
- Social customs
- Survival tips on laws, disease, crime, and how to stay out of trouble
- Typical business practices such as hours and rate of pay
- Opportunities for spouse employment

- Housing, health facilities, and schools
- Practical matters such as currency, transportation, telephones, time zones, and the measurement system
- Security

And often the list includes information useful in preparing for the assignment:

- Passports, visas, work permits; heath, tax and legal clearances
- Tax information
- Required immunizations
- How to send funds
- What to take and leave at home

Sometimes the list includes information specific to the particular assignment or project. The following is adapted from Harris and Moran:[8]

- The overseas job environment and organization
- The clients, contractors, and key personnel
- The work schedule and hours
- Hiring procedures
- Contract monitoring
- Project procedures and progress reports
- Quality control
- Job-site security
- Labor relations
- The host attitude toward the project or organization
- Necessary technical training

These lists are certainly not exhaustive, and any given assignment may require more or less information. And keep in mind that much of the information described about the host culture and ecology is also useful to have about home prior to

---

8. Harris, P. R., & Moran, R. T. (1987). *Managing cultural differences.* Houston: Gulf.

returning to ease that return and the reentry shock associated with it.

The actual list for a particular assignment depends on the assignment ecology involved. If, for instance, it is a marketing assignment, then it might be good to be aware of these general suggestions provided by Copeland and Griggs:[9]

- "The fact is that ancient differences in national tastes or modes of doing business are not disappearing." If we don't attend to these differences, we will make mist?kes and it will cost us money.
- "Even on a clear day, you can't see Belgium from New York." We must go there and learn the market; the biggest error is failingto get enough information about the custormer.
- "Sell to the customer (who that is, is not always obvious)." We must sell to the decision maker, and decision makers differ from country to country and industry to industry.
- "Identify national goals; promote national pride." Nationalism is growing, not disappearing: we must be sensitive to it.
- "Don't go it alone in unfamiliar territory." Get the best guide we can.

Or if the assignment is to develop an advertising program, they suggest:[10]

- "You may adopt or ditch entirely the local style, but you'd better know what it is."
- "Appeal to the right need with the right benefits."
- "Reflect the right values in the context of the ad."
- "A rose by any other name would not sell so well because it would not have the centuries of poetic propaganda and customer satisfaction behind it."

---

9. From L. Copeland & L. Griggs, *Going international: How to make friends and deal effectively in the global marketplace.* Copyright © 1985 by Random House, Inc.

10. Ibid., pp. 59–65.

- "Colors and symbols have meaning, often not the ones you think."
- "Watch out for restrictions."
- "Don't overlook practical problems.' Watch for poor printing, unreliable mail, no TV.

Sometimes the information in an orientation program is provided to assigned personnel by the organization, sometimes by contracted firms or consultants, and sometimes the personnel are simply guided in seeking it out on their own. Many do the latter, whether advised to or not. There are several sources of information useful for orientation at the national and organizational levels on which the foregoing lists have primarily focused:

- *Public* and *university libraries* contain a vast amount of printed and video materials about most assignment sites. They have historical, economic, political, and cultural information. There are good books written specifically for those going on international assignments to specific sites that have information useful for orientation. Useful material doesn't include just nonfiction. Often a novel set in the host culture can be a wealth of information—we have the benefit of a great deal of on-site research by the author in preparing the book.
- Many good *organizational libraries* have collected material both specific to the assignment sites in which their personnel most commonly do business and specific to their demonstrated information needs. The U.S. Navy, for instance, has well-organized and attractively presented material on all sites to which naval personnel are frequently deployed.
- Several *periodicals* and *in-flight magazines* either focus exclusively on the concerns of those on international assignments (*The International Assignment* and *The International Business Travelers' News*) or address concerns common to all travelers (*Signature*). A typical issue of *The International Assignment*[11] dealt with

---

11. *The International Assignment* (July 1987).

"The hassles of hustlers," "What conversion tables don't tell about metrics," "The traveler and his/her money," "Controls on foreigners in China," "Direct dialing to the USA," "Adjusting to the Middle East," "Uncle Sam and international marriage," "Men's clubs and discrimination," "Six questions to ask the school," and a special article on "Venezuela."

- *Newspapers, news magazines,* and *films* from both home and abroad present a great deal of contemporary political, business, social, and cultural information.
- Many national *governments* provide information about overseas sites to help their citizens do business internationally (for example, the U.S. and Foreign Commercial Service of the International Trade Administration of the Department of Commerce) and provide information about their own country to help foreign companies do business there (various embassies, consulates, and trade missions).
- More and more frequently *travel agents, travel consultants, airlines,* or even *credit or charge card companies* provide useful information (Thomas Cook, American Express, Visa, Mastercard, Diners, and so forth).
- Returning *compatriots* who have spent time in the assignment site can be useful and, of course, those in one's own organization who have been on a similar assignment to the same site are potentially very useful. We should guard, however, against relying too much on them—they are not us and their assignment was not ours!
- *Visitors* from the assignment site—businesspersons, university faculty, international students, or even tourists can be useful sources of information.

### The Role in Managing International Assignments

The range of information available and potentially useful for orientation is enormous. But, as noted earlier, orientation programs commonly suffer from ambiguity or inconsistency in specifying criteria of assignment effectiveness and thus a lack of clarity about what information those on international assignments most need. In terms of the dual objectives of managing international assignments identified earlier in this chapter the following are the key *roles* of orientation:

- *Providing information that assists personnel to develop more accurate perceptions of the host culture and assignment ecology and thus reduces the frequency and severity of ecoshock.* For instance, if we know ahead of time that we are going to encounter difficulty in *quickly* establishing anything but superficial relationships in Hawaii—the land of "Aloha"—then we are likely to be less confused and frustrated by the *realities* of an island ecology.
- *Providing information that assists personnel in identifying tasks they will encounter and ecological characteristics most likely important in those tasks and expanding their awareness of alternative ways to do business effectively in them.* The latter would involve familiarizing them with the ways of doing business in the host culture and thus the skills and expectations hosts are likely to bring to the tasks with them.

It is these roles that should guide orientation programs in terms of defining both the kinds of information that would be most usefully provided and the sources from which to get that information.

In specifying both these roles, emphasis is on providing information about the host culture and ecology at the national and organizational level. Again, the reason is that those are usually the only levels at which reliable information is available to the organization prior to assignments. The information potentially most valuable—information about the actual task ecologies which will be encountered on a particular assignment—is nearly always sketchy at best, often simply unavailable. We may know something ahead of time about the man we must see to get a distribution contract and the place the meeting will be held, but that's about it. That's why a sense of presence is so critical to international assignments.

## A FINAL NOTE

Good orientation can give us some idea about what an assignment will involve; it can help us narrow the range of ecological characteristics to look for a bit, it can help us identify a broader range of alternative ways to do business, but in the end we're always on our own. *It's we who must, while sitting there facing our partner or adversary, see the actual ecology of the task and see the best way to complete it effectively.* It is to training for these skills that we turn next.

# TRAINING

Chapter 9

**Training programs** provide skills deemed necessary on an assignment to complete it successfully. Thus, the chief distinction made here between *orientation* and *training* is that the former involves *information* and the latter involves *skills*.[1,2] This distinction is not always made, however, and we often see the terms "cross-cultural orientation" and "cross-cultural training" used interchangeably. The distinction is useful, though, because orientation and training programs play quite different roles in strategies for managing international assignments. As we have seen, for instance, at least some orientation is necessary as part of screening and self-selection prior to identification of those actually to be assigned; training need not take that place in the management sequence.

Training provides both cognitive and behavioral skills. It is probably the most developed of the management programs associated with international assignments, and in some cases the two are viewed as programmatically equivalent. There are three traditional types of training associated with three general categories of skills typically thought to be important on international assignments: **technical** or **professional training, language training**, and **culture training**. As noted in Chapter 4, their respective emphasis depends a great deal on the organization's orientation to doing business. For those with the "people everywhere are the same" and "our way is best" orientations, the emphasis has been on technical and language training; for those with the "we must do it their way" and "we must compromise" orientations, there has been at least some emphasis on culture training.

1. Bennett, J. M. (1986). Modes of cross-cultural training: Conceptualizing cross-cultural training as education. *International Journal of Intercultural Relations, 10*, 117–134.

2. Kohls, L. R. (1987). Four traditional approaches to developing cross-cultural preparedness in adults: Education, training, orientation, and briefing. *International Journal of Intercultural Relations, 11*, 89–106.

# TECHNICAL OR PROFESSIONAL TRAINING

Personnel assigned internationally certainly need the appropriate technical and professional skills associated with their business. These may be management skills, engineering skills, consulting skills, teaching skills, research skills, financial skills, athletic skills, or artistic skills. In years past, it may sometimes have been the case that those *without* the highest level of such skills were "exiled" to an international assignment as a means of getting them out of the home office where they could do real damage! Or it was commonly the case that those with the skills wouldn't go: they would see such assignments as "death blows" to their careers!

Those were the days when the international activities of organizations were often quite tangential to the main operations. As indicated in Chapter 1, that is *not* typically the case in today's world. International activities are now commonly a major operation. Thus it is now the *most* competent—not the least competent—that must be sent internationally.

Yet despite the importance of doing business internationally, new or inexperienced personnel are still sent abroad to get "experience" prior to coming home to do the "real" work in the organization. A partial reason for this practice may be ethnocentricity in those in the home office: clients, customers, partners, and so forth from other cultures aren't perceived as sophisticated, as educated, as technically competent, or as professional. Thus there is sometimes an expectation that the organization can get away with sending less competent people there. In most instances, that simply isn't the case. While sometimes the host country may be less developed, the *specific people* that we deal with are often *very* competent. They are frequently the "cream of the crop" in terms of education, training, and experience. And they expect us to be at least equally so!

Hosts view themselves as being important so, of course, they expect that our organization would only send the very best to do business with them. Their expectations for *our* competence are often unrealistically high, considering the added difficulties associated with such assignments described throughout this book. For example, however technically or professionally competent we are, after two weeks on an international assignment we will be very tired, suffering from ecoshock, frustrated with the interpreters, and missing our children. Believe me, our competence just isn't going to come through at the same level it does back home!

Thus international assignments often present a "loaded" situation: the "sending" organization may send someone of *less* technical competence, and the "receiving" organization expects someone of *more* competence! There is a gap between expectations and reality. To some extent, the gap can be lessened by good screening and self-selection: the best possible people need to be sent. But a technical or professional training program may need to be utilized to assure the highest possible level of competence for those who—for whatever reason—actually go.

## LANGUAGE TRAINING

If you ask people—particularly people *without* a lot of international experience—what the biggest problem on an international assignment is, they will commonly say "language." Most managers say that. And that's in part why probably 98 percent of training for international assignments in Japan and Europe is principally language training. In the United States the percentage is somewhat lower, probably because Americans expect others to understand English or because they have simply given up trying to motivate and train personnel to reach acceptable competence in any foreign language.

It is not clear, however, that language differences are the biggest problems. Often it is *after* they are resolved through our learning their language or they ours or through adequate interpretation that the *big* problems of doing business begin. But those differences are certainly the biggest *initial* problems faced on international assignments. And a strategy for managing assignments needs to involve a language training program. Communication is central to doing business and communication requires a shared language.

Language training is as specialized, varied, and sophisticated as technical or professional training, and an in-depth presentation of it is beyond the scope of this book. However, it needs to be stressed that the ability to speak some of the language of the host country is valuable for a feeling of efficacy in living, if not working, there. Often, the evidence that we have even attempted to learn some of the hosts' language will be interpreted positively by the hosts as indicative of our good intent, a willingness to learn, and an egalitarian approach to the business at hand. Nevertheless, unless we speak their language very well, they would generally prefer to use our language (if they speak ours well) or rely on an interpreter.

Learning to speak a language well really requires education or socialization, not training. It is a "lifelong" not a "month-long" endeavor. Thus the objectives of language training must be realistic. We can realistically learn enough of the hosts' language in a training program to facilitate living in the country, produce a positive reaction from our hosts, and probably add a dimension to our feeling of self-reliance. And in understanding even a bit of the language, we may understand the host better and appreciate our interpreter more.

Language training can also provide skills for communicating more effectively in our own language with those for whom it is not primary: for example, communicating in English with those for whom English is a second or third language. Thus we can learn to speak more slowly; enunciate more clearly; and use less jargon, simpler sentences, more breaks, more examples, more visuals, and shorter sessions. And when listening we can learn to be more patient, refrain from interrupting our hosts, or completing their sentences for them. And we can learn to be more forgiving, attributing poor grammar or vocabulary to their lack of language competence rather than professional competence. We will find all these skills well appreciated because they show empathy, are not easy, and are rare internationally.

Given the complexities of doing international business, it is generally best to rely principally on interpreters for the important communication. Thus another concern of language training, and often more directly relevant to doing business effectively, is training in how *to select and use interpreters*. Being interpreters in international business situations is certainly one of the most challenging of jobs. Interpreters are more than just "translators." Few languages "translate" very well at the level of specificity at which most business is conducted. Interpreters are in the role of bridging cultures—of trying to understand the meaning of a message from one party and communicate a sufficiently similar meaning to the other party or the other party's interpreter. Interpreters must be aware of the *perspectives* of all the participants to communicate *information* from one to the other. They may be major sources of "on-the-spot" cross-cultural and intercultural training. Because of their job and experience, they may also be part of IMC networks. And they may play a key role in assisting participants develop IMCs.

## CULTURE TRAINING

The previous lack of clarity about the skills required for successful international assignments and the objectives for managing them has had a particularly big impact on cultural training. The clarification provided thus far in this book allows us to distinguish between *cross-cultural training* (training in how other cultures do business) and *intercultural training* (training in how to do business with other cultures). Most organizations have missed this distinction, and, as a consequence, programs have had mixtures of both without clearly specifying the objectives of either in terms of the management of assignments. The point has been made that programs have traditionally emphasized cross-cultural training and that that emphasis is misplaced. Further, most of the techniques used with this "training" actually provide much more information than they do skills, even though they might involve role playing or interaction. Finally, in terms of the *way* the training is provided, it's not uncommon for organizations to hire a trainer to "parachute in" to the home or overseas office, hit often unwilling personnel with some "culture" or "rules of thumb," and be flown out in one or two days. It's kind of a "counterinsurgency strategy" for managing what is essential to the organization's competitiveness.

Cross-cultural programs are, then, more orientation than training and would fill the same role as orientation in managing international assignments. That role, again, is primarily to assist personnel in developing more accurate perceptions of the host culture, become more accustomed to the differences, and thus reduce the frequency and the severity of ecoshock. It is secondarily to assist them somewhat in increasing their awareness of the assignment ecology and awareness of alternative ways to do business in it. The latter is achieved by familiarizing them with at least the hosts' ways.

**Intercultural training programs,** on the other hand, are more *skill* based and should play a central role in training along with technical and language training. *The role of intercultural training is to assist personnel in doing business effectively in different ecologies by helping them develop the sense of presence and the social, communication, and stress-management skills essential to establishing IMCs.*

The remainder of this chapter addresses issues associated with intercultural training that should help organizations to develop a more effective training program. Although the term "intercultural" is used here, we must keep in mind that, strictly speaking, culture is only one characteristic of the ecologies faced on international assignments. Although we are rather "saddled" with that terminology, the training referred to by the term should address the other characteristics as well.

### Training for a Sense of Presence

A sense of presence requires personnel to have an ecological awareness, an awareness of alternative ways of doing business, and seeing an alternative tailored to the ecology. Recall that it is termed a *sense* of presence because it is felt to be more perceptual or intuitive than analytical. As such it presents some real challenges for training.

Realistically, we cannot "give" people a sense of presence they can take away from training with them. Everyone has it at times, and the job of training is to assist them in having it, and applying it to doing business, at the *right times*: when needed to complete important tasks in different ecologies, when the "automatic pilot" or rules of thumb are not useful. Training can provide personnel with *increased* skills to better

1. Identify tasks that must be completed as part of a particular assignment.
2. Describe relevant characteristics of each task ecology.
3. Specify a range of perceptions associated with how to do business in each task and the degree to which each is supported by the task ecology.
4. Select strategies best supported by specific task ecologies and identify the perception-ecology links.

5. Monitor the effectiveness of selected strategies and modify them as necessary based on goodness-of-fit with the task ecology and changes in it.

One general technique involves confronting trainees with a sequence of "assignments." For example,

> You have been assigned to New Delhi to oversee the procurement and installation of new information processing/communication equipment for a subsidiary. Your organization expects the process to take about six months. You must rely on the subsidiary for clerical and other support. Your salary will be . . ., and so forth.

These can be descriptions of assignments presented in written or video formats, role-played assignments, or real assignments facing different trainees. They must be presented to trainees from the perspective of the need to understand the role of IMCs in doing business effectively. The "assignments" can vary in complexity from brief sketches to elaborated cases.

To facilitate developing skills for *1* and *2*, trainees should provide lists based on their assessments of the tasks and task ecologies, respectively. For *3*, trainees should provide a list of alternative strategies and then for each alternative return to *2* and alongside each ecological characteristic place a " + " if they think it supports the strategy, a " − " if it impedes the strategy, or a "0" if it is irrelevant to the strategy. The selected strategy identified in *4* should then be that with the best + to − ratio. The complexity of trainee responses should parallel the amount of realism or detail in the "assignments." Between each "assignment" there should be discussion of responses led by a facilitator.

*Assessment* of improvement in *1*, *2* and *3* over the course of the training program can be achieved simply by evaluating the increase in the length and clarity of the lists across successive "assignments." At the beginning of training, it is common for each of the lists to emerge with a lot of labor and include only obvious—but not necessarily important—tasks, ecological characteristics, and so forth. But over the course of training, lists typically come easier and become much more sophisticated. Additionally, for *2* a decrease in the proportion of 0s associated with alternative strategies should be noted. That is, trainees should get better at identifying the *relevant* ecological characteristics for each task.

Assessment of *4* is both quantitative and qualitative requiring evaluation of the improvement in + to − ratios and the ability to spell out the perception-ecology links for selected alternatives. Assessment of *5* is also quantitative and qualitative, requiring evaluation of the appropriateness of changes on items to changes in task ecologies presented in an "assignment." (Descriptions of some assignments include ecological change.) Worksheets useful in steps *1* through *5* are illustrated in Figure 9.1.

A more sophisticated extension of this technique can match items on the lists and the descriptions of perception-ecology links

Page 1
**ASSIGNMENT:** _____

Page 2
**TASKS** essential to Completion of Assignment
1. _____
2. _____
n. _____

Page 3
**ECOLOGICAL CHARACTERISTICS** of Task _____
1. _____
2. _____
n. _____

Page 4
**ALTERNATIVE PERCEPTIONS** for How to do Business in Task _____
1. _____
2. _____
n. _____

Page 5
**SELECTED STRATEGY** for Task _____
*(With "Perception-ecology" Links in Parentheses)*
1. _____
2. _____
n. _____

Page 6
**EVALUATION** of the Effectiveness of Strategy for Task _____
*(With suggested modifications to improve "Perception-Ecology" Links)*
+_____o_____-
1. _____
2. _____
n. _____

**Figure 9.1** Worksheets for Training in a Sense of Presence

with those of "experts"—people with demonstrated success in those types of assignments. This allows an estimate of the correspondence between the "tacit knowledge" of experts and that of trainees.

This general technique for training in a sense of presence can be very usefully complemented by techniques more traditionally associated with other types of cross-cultural or intercultural training. Some of the more relevant of these are described briefly in the paragraphs that follow.

***Self-awareness Training.*** This uses techniques to sensitize trainees to the cultural basis of their own perceptions and behavior. For Americans **contrast American episodes** are frequently used to help them better understand what commonly sets them apart from others when doing business.[3] The presumption is that the more we know the cultural basis of our own perceptions, the easier it is to *recognize* cultural differences when we encounter them and the more *accepting* of them we will be. Focus, then, is on the culture of the trainee, not the host. Members of "majority" or "dominant" cultures may particularly profit from self-awareness training because they have had less need to develop self-awareness previously: "minorities" exposed to at least two cultures (their own and the dominant culture) generally must have good insight into both to be successful.

***Attribution Training.*** This uses a technique called a **cultural assimilator** or **intercultural sensitizer**.[4] It involves presenting trainees with "critical incidents" of interaction difficulties commonly encountered in a *specific* culture, and the trainees must select among the alternative perceptions presented for each incident the one most typical of the hosts. The objective is to help trainees make the isomorphic attributions discussed in Chapter 6. Brislin and his colleagues have developed a *culture general assimilator* designed to assist trainees in interacting with *any*

---

3. Kraemer, A. J. (1969). The development of cultural self-awareness: Design of a program of instruction. Alexandria, VA: Human Resources Research Organization.

4. Albert, R. (1983). The intercultural sensitizer or culture assimilator: A cognitive approach. In D. Landis & R. W. Brislin (Eds.). *Handbook of intercultural training*, Vol. 2. New York: Pergamon.

other culture. This seems particularly promising for use in training for a sense of presence because it exposes trainees to a very wide variety of assignments, tasks, and ecological characteristics on which they can hone their skills. An item from it follows.

---

## A Manager's Dilemma

Ned Schwartz, the manager of a large factory in Canada, had been transferred to an operation of the same size in a Central American branch, as its production had always been low. Ned had a reputation of getting things done, but from the start Ned had a hard time. Government regulations made procuring needed materials difficult. Communication from his site to headquarters was slow and often garbled. Even Ned's personal work habits had to be changed. He was used to working late and inspecting the plant after most of the workers had gone home, but strict military rule imposed curfew hours over such installations as Ned's. In his own country there were organizations to protest such unreasonable restrictions, but superiors here said there was nothing one could do. Ned became increasingly depressed and ineffective. He finally asked to be sent back to his original operation.

What can help explain Ned's situation?

1. The job was not really appropriate for Ned since the difficulties were too great.
2. Ned found himself in a situation where he had relatively little control over matters.
3. Operations in Third World countries are impossible to bring to maximization given the resources available.
4. Ned did not have the proper local support. If he had been nicer to local authorities and workers, they would have offered him more cooperation.[5]

---

Trainees select the alternative they feel best describes the situation, are informed of why they are or are not correct (the best answer is 4), and try again or proceed to another situation.

Assimilators provide a self-paced, programmed learning tool in which if we know a lot already about a culture, or are a good

---

5. From *Intercultural interactions: A practical guide*, R. W. Brislin et al. Copyright © 1986. Sage Publications, Inc.

learner, we get through quickly. It has been more rigorously evaluated than any other culture training technique and appears to be useful with motivated trainees.

*Experiential or Simulation Training.* This provides trainees with experiences that in some ways simulate those they will likely encounter in a host culture. Typically, **stop-the-world** techniques are used: events occur that trainees don't expect; their perceptions are not verified.[6] The resulting ecoshock is experienced in a relatively safe, structured, supervised environment, and they learn to cope with it in ways that are effective for them. Many trainees simply do not fully accept the impact of cultural or ecological differences from more "cognitive" training alone. Not until their "world is stopped" do they begin to see and feel what they will confront on their assignment. And then they *are* motivated!

The success of experiential training relies heavily on guidance by a facilitator in relating the experience to assignment objectives, identifying differences in perception and behavior confronted, the problems produced by them, and alternative ways to deal most effectively with them. Without that guidance, it can become just the "fun and games" administrators typically view it as. With the guidance it can be very valuable.

*Interaction Training.* This is closely related to experiential training in that it provides stop-the-world experiences. In this. case, however, the experiences are provided in interaction with members of the host culture. The experiences that occur are generally much more similar to those that they will encounter on assignment. Trainees are "sent out" into that culture to complete some task: buying a hat in Tijuana or getting to the corporate office from the Narita airport outside Tokyo. They then return to the training session where again the success of the technique relies on guidance by the facilitator on those same issues described with experiential training.

---

6. Castaneda, C. (1972). *Journey to Ixtlan.* New York: Simon & Schuster.

## Training for Social Skills

The importance of social, communication, and stress-management skills is certainly not unique to international assignments. Training programs for each are well developed, and the program and research literatures associated with them are extensive and easily available. There is no particular reason to expect that training in them for international assignments needs to be unique. Thus the examination of issues associated with them here is very selective.

The key issue for social skills training for international assignments is that the behavioral strategies for developing, maintaining, and dissolving relationships that work well at home may not work at all well abroad. Or, even if they potentially could, the assignment ecology in terms of place, time, communication, stress, and so forth simply may limit their use. Thus we need to expand the range of alternative strategies with which we are practiced—that we can perform well—and then learn to select those most likely to work best in a particular business relationship.

The kinds of role playing, interactive exercises common in good "social skills" and "team-building" workshops are just what's needed to build up a repertoire of alternatives. Typically these exercises focus on behavioral strategies for dealing effectively with a range of relationship challenges. Among those singled out by Ratliffe and Hudson, for instance, are initiating relationships, relationship maintenance, building supportive climates, and managing interpersonal conflicts along with many of the communication strategies mentioned in Chapter 7.[7] In fact, communication and social skills are often merged in training programs. If role-playing exercises can be combined with video feedback and instructions for "rehearsal" following the training, so much the better.

Although it is not unusual for the trainer to press for adoption of a particular strategy as "best," we need not heed that advice. We, not our trainer, must be aware of the cultural or

---

7. Ratliffe, S. A., & Hudson, D. D. (1988). *Skill building for interpersonal competence*. New York: Holt, Rinehart and Winston.

ecological relativity of a strategy. We just need to take advantage of the opportunity to acquire and practice as many behaviors as we can.

In terms of then selecting the alternative strategy to use in a particular relationship, the generic social skills approach described in Chapter 6 is useful. It represents one of the more active training/intervention efforts in the social skills area, though it tends to be focused more on those seriously lacking in such skills than "normals" who need to improve them. As mentioned earlier, in most cases the duration of relationships and relative consistency of relationship ecologies allow for an iterative, feedback process to be effective. If not, then, we must again use our sense of presence.

### Training for Communication Skills

The key issue for communication skill training for international assignments is that, analogous to social skills, the strategies that are most commonly applicable at home and the behavioral styles associated with them may not work as well abroad. We need to expand the range of strategies and styles with which we are practiced and select those that seem to work best for *us* on *our* assignments. Again, the role-playing, interactive exercises mentioned earlier are what's needed to build up a repertoire.

In terms of communicating in *particular tasks* on assignments, we have an additional problem, however, of determining which types of communication strategies are required: ritual matching, perspective sharing, agenda matching, information exchange, or social influence. The need for one or more of these depends on the task ecology. Perceptions of that need constitute an important dimension of an IMC. We have seen already, though, that ritual matching, perspective sharing, and agenda matching are often particularly critical in those ecologies. Training programs in communication skills for assignments need to pay special attention to them.

Table 9.1 provides an illustration of some appropriate perception-ecology links in terms of communication-related perceptions. The chief skill in identifying such links, as with others for how to do business, is a sense of presence. Thus *training in communication skills and a sense of presence should be well integrated.*

**TABLE 9.1** Communication Skills for International Assignments

| Ecology | Communication-Related Perception |
|---|---|
| Are participants familiar with one another? | |
| Yes: | Information exchange; high-context communication. |
| No: | Perspective sharing; low-context communication. |
| Are participants similar to one another? | |
| Yes: | Information exchange; high-context communication. |
| No: | Perspective sharing; low-context communication. |
| Don't know: | Ritual matching. |
| Do participants have similar objectives? | |
| Yes: | Proceed as normal. |
| No: | Engage in agenda matching. |
| Don't know: | Perspective sharing. |
| Is the task familiar to participants? | |
| Yes: | Concentrate on attention. |
| No: | Concentrate on presence. |
| Is the task structured? | |
| Yes: | Concentrate on attention. |
| No: | Concentrate on presence; agenda matching. |
| Is there a time constraint? | |
| Yes: | Efficient ritual and perspective sharing if necessary; high-context communication if possible. |
| No: | More elaborate ritual and, perspective sharing if necessary; low-context communication possible. |
| Is power formally distributed? | |
| Yes: | Proceed as normal. |
| No: | Engage in agenda matching. |
| Does the task involve high stress? | |
| Yes: | Concentrate on attention and/or presence. |
| No: | Watch for lapses of attention or presence. |

## Training for Stress-Management Skills

As with social and communication skills, there is a large range of training programs and associated literature on stress management. Programs directed particularly at "executives" have been, and will continue to be, among the more popular on the workshop/seminar circuit. Again because the stress associated with international assignments (both from ecoshock and "normal" stressors associated with doing business) is physiologically the same stuff as it is domestically, many of those programs are applicable.

Programs typically describe to participants what stress is, what causes it, what its personal and professional consequences are, and ways to manage it. Some programs present stress-management *panaceas* which can be grouped in a number of categories: drugs, biofeedback, meditation and relaxation, exercise, diet, time management, and psychotherapy. Like other rules of thumb, some work for us in our ecology and some don't. Others provide an assessment of stressors and presentation of stress-management techniques more tailored to individual participant's needs and resources. This tailoring is necessary. We need a more *generic* approach to stress-management training, as well, in which we can:

1. Assess the source of the stress.
2. Identify a broad range of alternative coping strategies.
3. Select a strategy appropriate to our assessment of the stressors and our own personality, organizational ecology, and resources.
4. Practice and do it.
5. Evaluate its effectiveness.

One approach compatible with this generic one involves a **mediational model** of stress. This model specifies that *physiological arousal* is a necessary part of stress but that the *stressor situation*, *mental appraisal* of that situation and the arousal it produces, and the *coping response* are important as well.[8] In the context of international assignments stress-management intervention can then occur at any component of the model as illustrated:

### Stressor Situation
- Changing the situation by adding music, lowering noise, change workloads.
- Leaving the situation through transfer, vacation, or resignation.
- Increasing organizational support, particularly from the boss.
- Changing responsibilities.
- Getting more control over the situation.

### Mental Appraisal
- Redefining the severity of the stressor.
- Evaluating the stressor more positively.
- And, critical to ecoshock, understanding ecological differences that produce stress.

### Physiological Arousal
- Muscle relaxation.
- Meditation.
- Exercise.
- Prescription drugs and alcohol, coffee, and tea.

### Coping Response
- Improving technical and professional skills.
- Improving language skills.
- Improving a sense of presence.
- Improving social and communication skills.

Training then requires helping personnel build an *integrated coping response* appropriate to *them* involving intervention in all or most of these components.[9] Most commonly, this strategy

---

8. Smith, R. E. (1980). Development of an integrative coping response through cognitive-affective stress management training. In I. G. Sarason & C. D. Spielberger (Eds.), *Stress and anxiety*, Vol. 7. New York: John Wiley.
9. Ibid.

involves some plan of action, like any other business objective, that extends well beyond the duration of training and places the interventions in the job ecology. The flexible and "tailored" nature of this approach makes it ideally suited for the varied, yet stressful, ecologies typically faced on international assignments— particularly if combined with the generic approach suggested previously.

## OTHER TRAINING CONCERNS

There are several other concerns commonly encountered in developing a training program as part of a broader strategy for managing international assignments. Some of the more important of these are presented next in the form of questions. The answer to each question depends on the management strategy the organization selects. But *each* deserves careful consideration.

### Should Training Be *Culture Specific* or *Culture General*?

**Culture-specific training** is focused on a specific other culture or set of cultures: American, Japanese, French, Filipino, and so forth. **Culture-general training** is not focused on a particular culture but is designed to be applicable to *any* culture encountered on an assignment. Culture-specific training is most useful when we know the specific cultures we are going do business with on an assignment, we are going to be there for some time, and the way for doing business there is known. Culture-general training is most useful when we don't know the specific cultures we are going to do business with, there are simply too many of them feasibly to get culture specific training for each, or the ways they do business are not known.

Culture-specific training is usually more popular with trainees about ready for departure since they are often anxious and want specific, concrete lists of do's and don'ts upon which they can rely. Simple possession of such lists (however misleading) seems to reduce anxiety (until they find out they're misleading!). Culture-general training is more popular with those having no immediate assignment plans or having been abroad for some time. For the former, culture specific training seems irrelevant; the latter see how inaccurate it often is and the need for an alternative. Intercultural training programs might most often be culture general since the skills necessary to develop IMCs would appear to be broadly applicable. However, ecological characteristics and alternative ways of doing business relevant to a sense of presence, and social, communication, and stress-management skills may be somewhat culturally specific and require some culture-specific intercultural training as part of the program.

### Who Should Receive Training?

Just the assigned personnel, themselves? Or also the hosts they work with directly? Or the managers responsible for them? Or the family relocated with them? Or the family left back home? And should these different people be trained separately or together?

### Who Should Provide Training?

Is training provided by their own organization, the host organization, or both? Is it provided "in house" by staff trainers or contracted to "outside" specialists?

### What Should Be the Duration of Training?

Two hours, a day, a week, a month, six months, two years? "Full-time" and intensive or "part-time" and extended?

### How Should Training Be Provided?

Should technical, language, and intercultural training be independent or integrated? Successive or simultaneous? Provided by the same or different trainers?

### Where Should Training Take Place?

In the home country, in the host county, in some intermediate stopover point that is kind of like home and kind of like the host ecology? Should it be in the workplace or in retreats or in hotels or in specialized training facilities?

### When Should Training Take Place?

Before departure, in transit, after arrival? Should there be "booster sessions" during the assignment? Should there be re-entry training prior to the return? Should there be readjustment training after the return home?

## SOME FINAL NOTES

What should we expect? What is a realistic estimate of the effectiveness of training whether technical, language, or intercultural? In attempting to get an answer we must remember the *third theme* of this book that training (or any other program) alone is not adequate preparation for successful international assignments. That success requires the management of most or all of the programs described. If that is done, it's difficult to isolate the impact of training alone.

That having been said, we must be warned that people may often be *less* effective *immediately after* training than they were before—especially in intercultural skills and if "acceptance" by hosts is one criterion of effectiveness.[10] Typically, trainees are *sensitized to difficulties* by training, adding to their stress and disrupting their normal, practiced social and communication skills. They can become overly sensitive, overly cautious, clumsy people. They can manifest "posttraining paralysis." Training takes away old styles and presents new ones. It takes time and work to *practice* and *coordinate* these new styles and *integrate* them into our repertoire. Training is not a pill we "pop" and become all better. Training only helps us find what we need to do and, at best, gives us some practice in it. The real work of building skills occurs *after* the training sessions, not during them. It occurs on the job. And it takes time.

---

10. Weldon, D. E., Carston, D. E., Rissman, A. K., Slobodin, L., & Triandis, H. C. (1975). A laboratory test of effects of culture assimilator training. *Journal of Personality and Social Psychology*, 32, 300–310.

Finally, objectives for training must be *realistic*. We must remember that training can never *create* good marketers, or managers, or diplomats, or negotiators, or consultants. As noted earlier, we cannot take the negotia*tor* out of negotia*tion*. We can *never* replace in training a career of experience. But we can train *everybody*, so motivated, to be better.

# ARRANGING TRAVEL, ACCOMMODATION, AND SUPPORT

# Chapter 10

Some of the *most* obvious, but *least* emphasized, aspects of international assignments are those associated with travel, accommodation, and support. The first is particularly important for those on relatively short and/or frequent assignments in which time spent traveling can be the major component of the assignment: not only in-flight time, but preparing for flight, going to the airport, checking in, waiting for the flight, collecting luggage on arrival and going through immigration and customs, getting to the hotel, checking into the hotel, packing to leave, checking out, getting back to the airport, and waiting for the next flight. They are part of the assignment tasks and ecologies as well. How we deal with them can have a lot to do with how well we do business. When we arrive at the hotel (on short-term assignments) or an apartment or house (on longer ones), it becomes our new home and, often, office. They both are just as important to our doing business as they were back home. And at least as important as they is the support we receive from our organization, family, and associates—those with us and those back home.

## TRAVEL

Travel is, itself, stressful independent of changes in place, people, communication, and other characteristics of the ecology that produce ecoshock. It can also be physically strenuous and tiring. Perhaps nothing can erode a sense of presence more effectively than "jet lag"—we feel thickheaded, distant, and just "absent." So, assisting personnel with travel must be included as a program in the organization's strategy for managing international assignments. This is especially true if assigned personnel must travel every day or two with little opportunity for *rest*, much less adaptation. We rarely get training in how to travel.

There are issues associated with travel that are common across different modes—jet, rail, bus, ship—and issues that distinguish between them. The emphasis here, however, is on *jet travel*, since that is far and away the most frequent form of travel associated with most international assignments. Many travel-related issues are part of orientation: when to travel, which airline and flight to book, what to pack, and so forth. The focus here, though, is on the experience of jet travel and its impact on assignment effectiveness: the focus is on jet **lag**.

## What Is Jet Lag?

Jet lag (or more technically *travel dysrhythmia*) is produced by disruption of our body's circadian rhythms by changes in the light-dark cycle produced by travel across one or more (most significantly three or more) time zones in a short period of time.[1-3] The effect is usually greater traveling east than west, presumably because of the lost sleep. In a recent study of flyers between Los Angeles and Tokyo and between New York and London, 94 percent reported experiencing jet lag, 45 percent said it was severe, but only 56 percent reported doing anything to avoid or alleviate its symptoms.[4] Symptoms typically involve feeling sleepy when we shouldn't be sleepy, feeling wide awake when we should be sleepy, or being fatigued when we've done nothing tiring. We are unable to stay mentally alert and may lose our short-term memory and ability to solve even simple mathematical problems. We feel confused and exhausted, have headaches and constipation, and stumble in clumsiness. And this is all happening as we get off the plane and begin to do business—at the time we need to be at our best!

This is a bad time to negotiate a critical contract, meet an important dignitary, or make a complex decision. It may be a bad time to do anything but sit in the hotel lobby, do isometrics, or stroll around the neighborhood. As noted, *nothing* can destroy

---

1. Goldberg, V. (1977). What can we do about jet lag? *Psychology Today*, August, 70–72.

2. Minors, D. S., & Waterhouse, J. M. (1988). Avoiding jet lag again. *Nature, 332*, 23–24.

3. Mrosovsky, N., & Salmon, P. A. (1987). A behavioural method for accelerating re-entrainment of rhythms to new light-dark cycles. *Nature, 330*, 372–373.

4. R. L. Associates. (1987). Incidence, severity, and persistence of jet lag. Final Report of research conducted for Manning, Selvage & Lee, Public Relations, and the Upjohn Company.

a sense of presence quicker—or our ability to deal with relationships, communication, and stress. Given their role in doing business effectively, the implications of jet lag for successful international assignments should be apparent. Even presidents take notice. Former President Reagan was reported by his press secretary to have stopped over in Finland for four days to recover from jet lag prior to his "summit conference" with Soviet leader Mikhail Gorbachev in Moscow.

Many of our physiological processes occur in rhythms that respond to a 24-hour, light-dark cycle. Some of the more important rhythms are presented here along with effects of their disruption:

- *Eating and sleeping.* These are the disruptions that are most obvious to us. We can be caught hungry or tired when in a board of directors' meeting, or not hungry afterward with them at dinner, or not sleepy that night! If we are unable to sleep that night we will be even more tired the next day.
- *Body temperature.* Our capacity for peak performance and our "favorite" time of day often coincide with the high point in our body temperature. Normally this temperature is low in the morning and high in the late afternoon. On an international assignment, it may be at its highest when we are trying to sleep and its lowest when we need to do business. When everyone else is at their peak we may be like a reptile—out of heat, and looking for a warm rock.
- *Kidney functioning.* The formation of urine follows a cycle as well and is maximal during the day and minimal at night. Continuous trips to the toilet in the "new night" overseas will make sleep still more difficult.
- *Liver functioning.* The liver stores and regulates glucose, which is broken down to produce energy we need to live and work. This occurs primarily over the course of the daytime and is greatly reduced at night. By early morning our liver has used up most of its reserves, blood sugar levels fall, and (if we are awake) we usually become irritable, depressed, or anxious. In a different time zone we *are* often awake, and these ef-

fects are not welcome. Worse, we may misattribute the feelings to *events* during the day rather than physiology—making ecoshock even worse!

While we may adjust to disruptions in eating and sleeping in a few days, disruptions in other functions may take much longer. There appears to be a great deal of individual variation in the effects of jet lag. Those leading more irregular life-styles (airline flight personnel, for instance) or exposed to very different light-dark cycles (Eskimos) seem to experience milder effects.[5] While much remains to be learned about jet lag, its impact on doing business should not be taken lightly—whether diplomat or athlete!

### How Can We Cope with Jet Lag?

There are lots of rules of thumb and "promising cures" for jet lag and very little research to support them. Some of the more popular are presented here because, without the research, we all need to experiment ourselves to find what works best for *us*.

- *Adapt* our body to the time zone of our destination prior to departure. This involves scheduling meals, activities, and sleep in terms of the time at the destination: we eat dinner when it's 7:00 P.M. in our Honolulu destination even if that's 1:00 P.M. at home in Hong Kong. This strategy is useful if there simply isn't time for adaptation at the destination prior to doing important business. It may obviously, however, make things difficult before we leave. So the question becomes: "Which is more important?"
- *Rest* and *relax* before we leave, don't schedule major deadlines for just prior to departure, don't rush to the airport.
- *Schedule our arrival* as close as possible to our normal bedtime so we can more easily sleep and at least start off rested.

---

5. Goldberg. What can we do about jet lag?

- *Relax* on the flight and *don't* work or socialize much—both inhibit relaxation. We should *not* save our preparation for the assignment for those long hours on the plane—however tempting that block of time is and useful laptop PCs are. Such work only adds to the stress.
- *Wear warm and comfortable clothing* so we can rest more easily and, if convenient, sleep.
- *Avoid* heavy meals. Stay away from cigarettes and alcohol—the effects of both are exaggerated when flying.
- *Stroll* around the plane to stretch muscles and aid circulation, but we shouldn't turn the aisles into a jogging track.
- *Be prepared for arrival* by knowing about customs, immigration, and transportation to the hotel. We most definitely should have a hotel or other accommodation arranged at least for the night of our arrival! Not knowing where we will sleep, eat, or use the toilet can be major sources of anxiety.
- After arrival we should *sleep* if the timing is right, or *exercise, stroll* around the hotel, or *familiarize* ourselves with the neighborhood. These activities can reduce stress and help take our minds off the initial symptoms of jet lag. But we shouldn't try to do too much.
- It can be useful to *arrive earlier* than we announce to give ourselves time to get our bearings and adjust. We may not want to even inform our hosts of our arrival or departure dates. Hosts have been known to use this information in planning *their* strategies for doing business: they can take advantage of our jet lag by scheduling meetings when we are fatigued, or they can bring up major issues at the end of negotiations near our impending departure so we have no time to argue!

Recently, there has been interest in the value of certain drugs (Melatonin, for instance) in reducing *feelings* of jet lag, artificial manipulation of light-dark cycles to *forestall* it, and exercise at the normal sleep time to *speed up readjustment*. While all three seem promising, there simply is not adequate research yet as to their effectiveness. In fairness, however, I should reiterate that the previous suggestions are made by various authors based more on common sense or "informal observation" than on research, too. The most important advice in coping with jet lag is to *expect* it, learn to *recognize* it when it occurs, *plan* around it, and *attribute* the symptoms of it appropriately. We must attribute our fatigue, irritability, poor thinking, and so forth to their proper source, *not* to our own lack of competence or our hosts' manners. *But* we must remember that our hosts will rarely attribute our reactions to jet lag! The long flight is *not* the most salient thing in their minds. They are most likely to attribute our reactions to *us*, and we should be prepared for that as well: we can't get away with saying "give me a week or two for my cycles to adjust"—especially if they are paying for it.

When traveling, we mustn't forget our sense of presence either. A colleague waiting for a long flight with me in an airport departure lounge—and having apparently more sense of presence than I—noted the congealing of a particular configuration of ecological characteristics. It was an early morning and the ticketing agent was dealing with presumably boring, routine preparatory details. She looked as if she could use a "hello" and some pleasant, personal, low-key chatting. My colleague noticed it and got up and chatted with her casually. He had with him a coupon for a ticket upgrade from *coach* to *first class*, but its applicability to the morning's flight was *highly questionable* and open to interpretation by any agent. But because he was congenial and only casually mentioned this upgrade possibility, the agent was able to continue the social dialogue by asking to see the coupon. She subsequently provided a favorable interpretation, and he received the upgrade. During the flight he could stretch his legs, reflect on a "competency boost," relax, and prepare for doing business on his arrival. I, as a consequence of my normal preflight "trance," arrived in a more humbled mood. While a sense of presence may require more energy than normally appropriate for the routine of most airline flights, it is also well worthwhile to bring it to bear when circumstances favor it!

## ACCOMMODATION

Selecting a place to stay can play a major role in adjusting to jet lag (that's *where* the symptoms take place), the severity of ecoshock, and the difficulty of doing business. It can help to make contact with IMC networks and facilitate the development of IMCs. Assisting personnel in selecting and arranging accommodations should be another program in the organization's strategy for managing international assignments. The focus here is with hotels, since they are the principal form of accommodation for those on short-term assignments and frequently the initial form for those on longer-term assignments.

### The Role of Hotels in Coping with Ecoshock

Commonly personnel who frequent a particular overseas destination return to the same hotel because its familiarity reduces ecoshock and lessens the adjustment period so that they can "get down to business" more quickly. They know the restaurants, the executive support facilities, the recreational facilities, the way to get to and from their places of business, and frequently even the hotel staff. When not familiar with the destination, experienced travelers are inclined to stay with a familiar hotel *chain* or at least a familiar *type* of hotel: the accommodation is familiar even if other characteristics of the assignment ecology are not.

One issue of concern is whether to choose an international hotel (Hilton, Hyatt, Sheraton, Holiday Inn, Peninsula, Mandarin, Westin, Otani, Novotel) or a locally owned or managed hotel. Considerations range from ease in making reservations, to familiarity, to business services, to the impression it makes on hosts. The latter may be more impressed by the international hotel, but prefer us to support the local economy by staying at a locally owned one.

**International hotels** often have the same services, decor, food, and facilities. It's often difficult to tell what country we're in from inside the hotel. Their identity is international, and they cater to the international business culture and provide appropriate choices—a Western restaurant, a Chinese restaurant, a local restaurant, with internationally popular drinks, newspapers, and gifts. They confront the visitor with minimal additional ecoshock beyond what he or she must face in doing business. For most that's enough. For frequent travelers who stay in the same international hotels, the hotel chain can become an "around the world home."

**Local hotels** have an identity principally in the host culture. They cater to those more immersed in that culture and may be more physically proximal to it and thus more convenient. They are sometimes less expensive, but require somewhat more adjustment and skill in getting necessary services. In local hotels we are entering the host culture even if it may be a rather accommodating part of it (no pun intended): things are done, look, and just feel a little differently. If the objective is to avoid ecoshock by minimizing the opportunity to confront ecological differences then this is *not* the best choice. If the objective is to begin understanding and dealing with these differences (perhaps because doing our business will inevitably require it), then this *is* a good choice: it's a safe place to start practicing, like an "interaction training exercise."

## The Role of Hotels in Doing Business Effectively

It's important to assure that persons on assignment are housed in the *right* hotels. "Right" here means the place where they can recover from jet lag, where there are adequate business support services, there are meeting rooms, and they can get access to the IMC networks. There are "right" and "wrong" hotels: places that are "in" and those that are not. And they change frequently—the international crowd moves around. Similarly, choice of a hotel is taken by our hosts to represent our status and that of our organization. Again, there are appropriate places to stay. We must talk to people returning about what the right places are and develop contacts in the host culture—the hosts *always* know what the *wrong* hotels are! If the organization has a "local manager," identifying the right hotels is his or her job.

Particularly in hot climates the availability of *working* climate control such as air conditioning is important. It keeps temperature constant so we don't have to adjust to that characteristic of the ecology and also keeps us from going through our suitcase of clothes in one day. The availability of *rapid* laundry facilities is also important. Clothes never survive travel nicely pressed, and we may have to wear them "first thing" the next morning. We make at least an initial impression on our hosts by our appearance. They are usually dressed immaculately because they have a support system behind them. As with our behavior, hosts rarely attribute our disheveled appearance to travel or accommodation hassles. If we arrive for our meeting with clothes looking like they just came out of our suitcase, we have a major "impression management" problem!

And we mustn't forget that even a brief stroll *outside* to a meeting down the road in either a rainy or hot, humid climate will assure that we arrive looking as though we swam. Best make sure the hotel is well served by taxis or limos or has covered or closed walkways to where we need to go. Remember, it's not uncommon to do business with hosts having little international assignment experience and thus little appreciation of the ecology of such assignments. As such they may seem humored by our behavior, but privately are rarely very forgiving of it.

Most large hotels, both local and international, are rapidly updating the kinds of business support they provide. Such support may include typing, photocopying, business card printing and translating, telex, computer, facsimile, teleconferencing, interpretation, meeting rooms, clerical assistance, special "executive floors" focused on the needs of those doing business, 24-hour concierge and room service, cars and drivers, health clubs, a full range of personal items to either replace those left behind or diminish the need to pack them at all, a variety of rapid check-in and check-out procedures, rooms designed both for sleeping and meeting, and locations suited to businesspersons as well as tourists.[6] These hotels can play a major facilitating role in international business. They are expensive for an individual's budget, but for organizations they provide support resources beyond those that could be easily arranged separately for each assignment. If the right hotel is selected, the cost is worth it.

We must not forget our sense of presence once we've checked into our hotel and are "off duty," either. In Manila I was jolted back to the present during a postarrival stroll by my more streetwise wife who noted that we were being followed by three rather obvious assailants! On an international assignment we are never any more "off duty" than we are at home. If anything, because of our lack of familiarity with the place and our high visibility, we must be *more* vigilant.

Finally, for those on very frequent short-term assignments, airports are a type of "accommodation" as well. We eat, sometimes shower and sleep, and frequently do business in them

---

6. Heath, C. (1987). Wooing the traveling exec. *Signature*, January, 90–98.

(as well as wait for flights). They, too, can play a role in doing business effectively, and more and more we are seeing the same type of standardization that reduces ecoshock and the same types of support services to facilitate doing business that hotels are providing.

# SUPPORT

There has been increasing recognition among researchers, consultants, and managers of the important impact support networks have on the success of international assignments.[7] More traditionally described networks include the organization for which we work and a variety of social groups. A brief look is now taken at each, along with support functions they typically provide.

### Organizational Support

Most everything described in these last three chapters constitutes direct organizational support for international assignments. That is, the organization needs a strategy for managing international assignments which provides programs for screening, self-selection, orientation, training, travel, accommodation, and other support. Beyond such a strategy the distinction between organizational and social support often becomes blurred. The organization, for instance, may provide us not only with training but with friends and entertainment. Generally, though, organizations provide additional support in terms of some or all of the following:[8-11]

---

7. Fontaine, G. (1986). Roles of social support systems in overseas relocation. *International Journal of Intercultural Relations, 10,* 361–378.

8. Brislin, R. W. (1981). *Cross-cultural encounters: Face-to-face interaction.* New York: Pergamon.

9. Copeland, L. & Griggs, L. (1985). *Going international: How to make friends and deal effectively in the global marketplace.* New York: Random House.

10. Harris, P. R., & Moran, R. T. (1987). *Managing cultural differences.* Houston: Gulf.

11. Mumford, S. J. (1983). The cross-cultural experience: The program manager's perspective. In D. Landis & R. W. Brislin (Eds.), *Handbook of intercultural training.* Vol. II: *Issues in training methodology.* New York: Pergamon.

- *Assistance in actual preparation* for an assignment in terms of:

  *Preparations for leaving home* (physical exams, immunizations, passports, visas, work permits, tax and financial requirements, and shipping household effects).

  *Preparations for travel* (tickets, hotel accommodation in transit, wardrobe, important documents, and watching for prohibited items and special regulations).

  *Preparations for living and working overseas* (finding a home, arranging the delivery of household effects, arranging household help, banking, telephone service, schools, transportation, membership in clubs and associations, security, legal and tax advice, and vacations and home stays).

- *A clear description of the assignment objectives*: the mission. This is very important because without it, personnel can get lost "out there in the provinces." With distance and the difficulty of communication with the home office, personnel can become more concerned with the "local" ecological demands than with their mission.

- *Appropriate status and recognition.* Even in today's more global world, personnel on international assignments are often on a peripheral tract for career advancement. While more and more businesses are going international, the international dimension of many is still relatively minor. Personnel "there" do different things, produce different products, require different skills, associate with different people, and are simply absent from the home office more than are their domestic counterparts. They need to be understood and given support in terms of recognition, status, and utilization of skills. More and more high-potential personnel are being encouraged to go international, but without that support, it won't be worthwhile for them. An international assignment must be a real part of the career path, and management potential must be considered in terms of skills for doing business internationally.

- *Incentives or compensation* in a variety of forms. These include a base salary at home country levels, a foreign service premium, a cost-of-living allowance, a housing allowance, an education allowance for dependents, tax equalization, and home leave.
- *Facilities, resources, and communication* required to do business effectively. Communication is often the key support requirement. It must allow for adequate perspective and information sharing and do so using media responsive to constraints of time, distance, and technological development.
- *Performance appraisal* based on *realistic* objectives for the assignment. So commonly success on international assignments is a very "mushy," ambiguous affair, while failure is very visible.[12] Success is expected, so it is failure that makes the news! Further, we must remember that doing international business simply takes longer to produce results and that "patience" is an essential organizational trait.
- *Understanding the special problems of international business.* This includes awareness of—and developing a means of dealing effectively with—all the characteristics which set international assignments apart from their domestic counterparts. Particular concern must often be with problems stemming from differences in perspective between the field and the home office and political pressures affecting international business.
- *Assistance in managing stress and fatigue* associated with doing business apart from ecoshock. This can consist of formal stress-management training as well as home stays, recreation, local vacations, and due consideration of the proper assignment duration.
- *Provide assistance in the reentry process.* Once the assignment is over it's in the best interests of both personnel and their organization that the return home is as smooth as possible. This is necessary either to facilitate a quick return to high productivity in the home

---

12. Brislin. *Cross-cultural encounters.*

office or the preparedness of personnel for the next assignment. A plan to make best use of returning personnel should be developed at the time of their selection, prior to departure.

- *Assistance with social support and essential services.* Usually the organization's residence at an international site is much more established than is that of individual personnel. As such it is both possible and desirable to institutionalize social support and the provision of services for its personnel and dependents. Assigning an expatriate family to help the newcomers, encouraging company clubs and recreational activities, and providing housing, food, security, and transportation are examples of assistance.

## Social Support

In some cases social support needs are directly related to those associated with the job (meeting people and establishing contacts). In many other instances the needs are different, and their impact on the job is less direct, though not necessarily less important. Social support can be provided by (1) home country support groups (our friends and family back home), (2) home culture support groups (our friends and family with us on the assignment), and (3) host country support groups (those from the country in which we are on assignment). These groups provide for some or all of the following needs:[13-16]

- *Resources* that we need to live and work effectively at the international site: money when a check hasn't arrived, food when we're sick of restaurants, transportation when our car breaks down, the clothes that protocol or custom demand when the shops are closed.

13. Albrecht, T. L., & Adelman, M. B. (1984). Social support and life stress: New directions for communication research. *Human Communication Research*, *11*(1), 3–32.

14. Brislin. *Cross-cultural encounters.*

15. Copeland & Griggs. *Going international.*

16. Fontaine. *Roles of social support.*

- *Information* about all aspects of living and working at the international site, as well as what's happening back home.

- *Guidance* on how to live and work in an international site and models to follow. The case can be made that most people aren't particularly good "learners," but they are very good "emulaters." The trick is, of course, to find the proper model to emulate: someone in a similar ecology with similar resources and who is successful!

- A *different perspective* from our own that we can use to assist us in dealing with events that occur on assignments. This is particularly true, of course, for host culture support groups whose perspective is often especially useful for interpreting intercultural problems.

- A *similar perspective* to our own that can validate our identity, maintain our confidence, and provide a feeling of being understood. We're OK, even if those people stare at us or laugh at us because we're brown people in a white place, or white people in a brown place, or blue-eyed people in a brown-eyed place, or brown-eyed people in a blue-eyed place.

- *People with whom we can compare our performance, satisfaction, and adjustment* on the assignment. Particularly useful for comparison are those in home culture support groups; particularly dangerous are those in home country support groups living and working in a very different ecology. We cannot constantly be making comparisons with home.

- *People with whom we can share responsibility and effort* for the tasks of living internationally. When we are too stressed or tired they can pick up the slack! The complexities and rigors of dealing effectively on international assignments require teamwork. We need help and we need rest.

- *Familiarity.* When the world seems so different, so unpredictable, so confusing, so *new*, a social support group can almost be like home. This is, of course, particularly true of home country support, but it is most often the home culture support group that is more accessible—

thus the bars, associations, and hotels where expatriates congregate.

- *Companionship.* Both the good and bad times are better when they are shared with others. Companionship doesn't necessarily mean "liking." On an international assignment we must place less emphasis on liking than back home where there are more choices.

## IMC Networks

There are three major ways in which support systems are related to international assignments: (1) one of the primary sources of stress produced by relocation is the disruption of social and organizational support, (2) one of the primary aids in coping with stress and doing business effectively internationally is the use of available support systems, and (3) support systems available internationally are often fewer in number and functioning more poorly because they, too, are under stress.[17] Groups under stress can sometimes be more pathological than helpful: they may wish to hinder our success so that their own poor performance looks better by comparison. They treat international business as a "zero-sum game."

What is lacking in many attempts to provide support (as with the other management programs examined) is a clear specification of the role of that support in terms of the dual objectives for managing international assignments presented in this book. The majority of both organizational and social support functions are primarily of help in coping with ecoshock. Some (particularly the organizational ones) are useful in providing a nurturing environment for doing business. What we need, though, is to utilize support better to help personnel *develop strategies for doing business in different ecologies.* With respect to this objective, the support that needs to be more fully understood and better utilized is that provided by **IMC networks.**

As first mentioned in Chapter 5, many of the members of particular IMCs are embedded in networks of others who commonly use an IMC strategy when doing business with one another: successful people tend to find each other! Participants in these

---

17. Ibid.

networks are not simply "cultural informants" or "in-culture resource persons" useful in understanding *Their Way*. They are the people who successfully do business with the hosts, and they are hosts with whom that business is successfully done.

While IMC networks may be most likely found in "third cultures," "international communities," "diplomatic communities," or "expatriate communities," they may exist outside them. And it is important to keep in mind that *an IMC network is not equated with those communities*: many, if not most, of the members of such communities commonly place more emphasis on the *Our Way*, *Their Way*, or *Compromise* strategies. Only a subset are likely to do business frequently using IMCs. But they are the subset within which commerce, diplomacy, technology transfer, or foreign study are most effectively done. They are the people we must seek out as partners, clients, and colleagues. They are the key support group for international assignments.

IMC networks have no "membership lists" or "cards" or "badges." The participants certainly don't call themselves by any such name. The *more* we do business using IMCs, the *more* we are a participant and the *more* useful we are to others. When I say we must make contact with IMC networks, I mean those people who frequently do business internationally with one another that way. They are sometimes identifiable by *reputation* ("If you're going to do business with company A you should get together with person X—he's easy to work with"), sometimes through *exploration* (talking to lots and lots of persons X, Y, and Z), sometimes through a *chance* meeting on the plane or in a cocktail lounge. Sometimes *intermediaries* will find them for us, and sometimes they will find us. We must be open to all these opportunities.

Knowing where to look to find IMC networks involves knowing the assignment ecology. In different ecologies we may look in different places. In the Philippines it may be professional societies like the Philippine Society for Training and Development. They are not typically members of the international community, but they have international experience and are often sensitive to the requirements of doing international business. In countries like Australia it might be in academic communities. They typically have much more international experience than, for instance, their American counterparts. In Indonesia it might be upper-level government employees, for a similar reason: they often have successfully obtained advanced degrees overseas. In some countries we might turn to the American Chamber of Commerce (or its counterpart). But we must be careful: just because a company is in a directory doesn't mean it's successful (directories quickly go out of date because companies quickly go out of business) and the person listed (usually an officer) isn't necessarily responsible for the company's success. Again, different ecologies imply different places to look.

Armed with the knowledge of the IMC strategy presented in this book we should begin to know the questions to ask when the opportunities to make contact with potential IMC network participants arise and the criteria to use in evaluating the responses we receive. As a helpful hint, when asked in some way how they approach doing business internationally, nearly everyone will initially respond with some version of the *Our Way, Their Way*, or *Compromise* strategies. It usually takes a bit more subtle probing to determine, for instance, if he or she *really* tries to do it *Their Way* (and thus probably *is not* an IMC network participant). Or if he or she in fact tries to take *Their Way* and many other characteristics of the assignment ecology into account in developing a strategy (and thus probably is a network participant). Much of this "probing" involves just the kinds of perspective-sharing skills referred to in Chapter 7.

Participants in different IMC networks commonly do not know one another. Nevertheless, network functions from site to site are often quite similar:

- The burden of developing new IMCs for every task by everyone involved in doing business on an international assignment would be hopelessly taxing on people who are already taxed to the limits by the other demands placed on them by such assignments. While it is nevertheless often necessary to do so, frequently IMC networks *serve as a reservoir of tested IMCs* that can be tapped when necessary.

- Further, many don't have the skills to develop a new IMC, the motivation to do it, or even the experience to know that it's useful. IMC networks *provide both guidance in, and sometimes even "licensing" of, ways to do business*. While information on the ways may not be checked out in libraries, it is exchanged in the seminars, bars, clubs, or restaurants frequented by the participants.

- Not only do IMC networks provide the ways to do business internationally, they can also *provide experienced people.* Otherwise, both visitor and host could search long and fruitlessly for a member of the other culture sufficiently sophisticated in international ways to do business effectively. They can provide a pool of the potential "partners," "third parties," "intermediaries," "local managers," "interpreters," or "informants" often so necessary for doing business effectively between cultures.

- IMC networks *provide the means of contact* (the cocktail party, the reception, the formal introduction, the informal lunch) and sometimes *the places* in which international business is conducted (the club, the bar, the home, the hotel meeting room, the campus).

- Given the range of alternative ways to do business internationally, there is always the unsettling possibility that the way it was done with this same country, company, or person on the last assignment will be very different from the way it could be done on this assignment. Further, there is the likelihood that whenever we do business with a different country, company, or person an entirely different IMC must be used. IMC networks *provide some measure of continuity* over time and place. Things will change, but not too fast—and somebody is usually there to fill us in.

- They *serve as a means of guiding newcomers* and allowing them to move more rapidly toward levels of performance required for doing business effectively than they ever could on their own.

In any major place of international business IMC networks develop. They make things easier and more interesting. In places where such networks have not gelled, effective business tends to be a transient phenomenon: sometimes it happens, sometimes it doesn't.

## Skills in Developing Support

Because of individual differences in support requirements and assignment ecologies, a *generic* approach to developing that support is again most useful. Elsewhere I present an approach[18] initially adapted from Steele[19] involving the following steps:

- *Identifying support needs at home* ("What needs do I have now?"). This involves identifying the range of organizational and social support needs that we have at home and the networks that are filling those needs. Identification of the needs we have now may seem obvious, but most of us never think through what our needs are beyond the obvious ones. This skill involves taking a good, honest look at our needs. Some of those needs will be the same overseas, but some may be different. It is useful literally to *list* them.

- *Identifying support needs on the assignment* ("What needs are going to be unfilled there given the conditions of my assignment?"). Rarely are all our support networks relocated with us. Most commonly we are relocated with some of them, parts of some of them, or none of them! This skill involves identifying which needs will then become unfilled as our networks are left behind and identifying additional support needs that will occur on the assignment. We must carefully assess the extent to which our current home country support groups will continue to provide support across time and distance, the communication channels available, and whether those relocated with us will continue the same level of support.

- *Identifying support networks available on the assignment* ("What potential support networks are available there for me?"). This involves identifying the support we're bringing with us (our family or our work team),

---

18. Ibid.

19. Steele, F. (1980). Defining and developing environmental competence. In C. P. Alderfer & C. L. Cooper (Eds.), *Advances in experimental social processes*. New York: John Wiley.

what our organization provides, what our hosts will provide, and what we can find for ourselves. We must carefully assess our assignment ecology and its implications for support available. We must identify as broad a range of alternative networks as possible: making contact with assistance centers, inquiring through sponsors or informal social contacts, monitoring newspapers or club notices, visiting recreational or educational facilities, asking, observing. We mustn't at this point evaluate them. Some may be similar to those back home, and some may be very different. Some that appear similar may have very different functions. A church back home may provide quite different support from one overseas. The same goes for our workmates or a tennis club. And some networks that appear different may have similar functions. Be open!

- *Matching unfilled needs with available networks* ("What will work for me?"). This is a key social skill for international assignments. It requires knowing ourselves, our needs, and what's available. And then matching available networks with those needs. One reason why people appear to live very different life-styles overseas is that they often find that they require very different support networks to fill their needs. One frequently hears the complaint from abroad that there is nothing to do and no one to do anything with. What is really meant is that there is nothing *familiar* to do and no one *familiar* to do it with!

- *Quick personalization* ("What makes me feel at home?"). To feel confident—an essential for establishing and maintaining relationships—we need to feel "at home" in the new ecology. And we must do it quickly after arrival. Some people can almost immediately make a place seem personal and have a sense of belonging. This is particularly important for those who must relocate frequently to very different ecologies.

Often our identity is based on ties to a city or organization or family. Apart from them, we feel adrift. To be effective in establishing support on international assignments, the basis of our identity must be more portable. But what is portable? Clothes that feel part of us—especially if business or our gender requires us to wear something different most the time (suits, saris, barongs, sarongs, jeans, muu muus, or shorts). Posters, tapes, photos, hobbies, sports, hiking, jogging, knitting, reading, pets, or our car can also work. Or being sure to take time for ourselves. But we must not go too far into this "identity maintenance": too much emphasis on who we were may inhibit seeing who we must be. We need a balance.

- *Establishing contact* ("How do I say 'hello'?"). Once appropriate social support networks have been selected, social skills in establishing contact with persons in them are important. Many formal networks have structured procedures to introduce newcomers into the group. In less formal networks, more skill is required. As we saw in Chapter 7, however, to the degree that interaction with *hosts* is necessary, the process can be difficult because of cultural differences in strategies of relationship formation—different cultures say "hello" in different ways!

- *Support system understanding* ("Don't blow it!"). Once contact has been made with appropriate support groups and significant interaction has been initiated, more detailed knowledge of the network is critical to maintain involvement. Internationally, home culture support groups may tolerate a lot of deviance because they need all the people they can get: it takes five for a basketball team, and they'll forgive you for anything but poor shooting! Host culture groups, however, may not need us at all, and with the first mistake they dissolve back into the city!

- *Going home* ("How can I say 'Good-bye'?"). We must always say "good-bye." But the *way* we do it is important. It will affect how they remember us and how they treat the next person who comes along on assignment. And international communities are small and mobile: we may run into the people elsewhere and need them, or they us.

Then there is the need to reestablish support back home. If the assignment has been a long one, the steps may be just the same as those on our assignment. Not infrequently, it is easier to establish *new* support networks back home, make new friends, than it is to rekindle old ones!

## A FINAL NOTE

We have examined several types of programs essential for meeting the dual objectives identified for managing international assignments: assisting personnel to cope with ecoshock and assisting them to develop effective strategies for doing business in the assignment ecologies. We have looked at screening, self-selection, orientation, training, travel, accommodation, and support. While each program provided alone can be of some use, I must reiterate that to best achieve those objectives, they must be *managed*—planned, organized, coordinated, integrated, and evaluated.

# SOME
## *FINAL*
## FINAL
## NOTES

# Chapter 11

# A SYNOPSIS

To be consistently successful on international assignments requires us to cope with the ecoshock produced by new assignment ecologies and to develop strategies for doing business effectively in them. While both challenges are important, the issues presented in this book have reflected an emphasis on the latter. These issues have been organized in terms of three major themes:

1. The key strategy for doing business effectively is to develop IMCs tailored to the ecology of specific tasks that must be completed as part of those assignments.
2. The primary skill required to develop these IMCs is a sense of presence.
3. International assignments must be managed to assist us in improving our sense of presence and social, communication, and stress-management skills and developing IMCs. This management involves planning, organizing, coordinating, integrating, and evaluating programs for screening, self-selection, orientation, training, travel, accommodation, and support.

These themes represent what we on assignment *must* do to be successful and what we and our organization *can* best do by way of preparation. But we must remember, the "person" can never be taken out of the assigment, can never be replaced with a formula. We can be nurtured, we can be provided with the best possible opportunity for success, but when we get off the plane—even with communication and support—it is we who must do the business.

## MANAGING INTER*CULTURAL* ASSIGNMENTS

Many of the issues presented in this book are as appropriate to domestic inter*cultural* assignments as they are international ones. Problems involved with multicultural organizations doing business with a multicultural local or national community are at least as significant as problems of doing business internationally. In commerce, government, tourism, transportation, communication, or the delivery of health, mental health, welfare, education, or justice sevices we are faced with doing business with people who differ in how they perceive that business should be done.

At home our "assignments" do not *typically* involve confronting as broad a range of ecological differences as we would internationally (though they might—Hawaii is probably *more* ecologically different from New York than is London). If we are at home with a customer, client, colleague, boss, subordinate, or government official, it is more commonly *differences in people* that are of concern, not problems of place, time, travel, communication, support, and structure. Differences that can be important include those in business culture, social culture, education and training, union and work force attitudes, and even appearance (see Figure 11.1). Again the term "culture" refers to

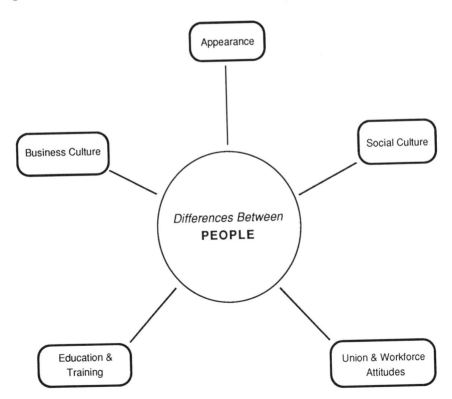

**Figure 11.1**  The Ecology of Cultural Diversity

shared perceptions that may stem from any common background (age, education, profession, and so forth), not just those based on race or ethnicity. Thus, at home the traditional term "culture shock" is *typically* more appropriate than is "ecoshock" (though not, perhaps, for a middle-class social worker from Utah working with refugees in Brooklyn).

But at home there is still the challenge of developing strategies for doing business effectively with other cultures. There is still the necessity of tailoring the ways of doing business to the cultural difference characteristic of task ecologies. The key strategy is the same, only now we might call it developing inter-*cultural* microcultures (fortunately, the acronym is also IMCs). The primary skill is still a sense of presence. Social, communication, and stress-management skills are still important. And the assignments must still be managed!

## MANAGING ORGANIZATIONAL CHANGE

I discussed in Chapters 2 and 3 that, while the relative ecological stability from one occurrence of a task to another and one type of a task to another allows for generalized ways of doing business (organizational cultures) to be useful, there are many occasions encountered domestically in which that stability disappears. Certainly that occurs when doing business internationally or inter-culturally. But we don't have to travel to Singapore or deliver social services to refugees at home to encounter ecological change. We don't need to purchase a ticket to *anywhere*. We can stay right at home, and our world, our organization, and our tasks will change around us. And the change is happening more rapidly all the time, driven by technological innovation; demographic trends; social, economic, and political transformations; and changes in markets, products, regulations, and organizational structures.

Historically our world has always been in transition. But the transition was relatively slow with opportunity for cultures to adapt to the change over the course of generations. These "adaptations" consisted of developing ways of doing things tailored to the ecological changes brought about by new technology and so forth. The adaptations were new rules of thumb at the level of organizational or national culture. People could be taught these "rules" and, because of the slow pace of transition, they were usually applicable over generations: we've had well over a dozen generations to adapt ways of doing busines to the ecological impact of the printing press.

But transitions are much more rapid now. We've had only a few generations to adapt to the telephone (in most places less), only a couple of generations to broadcast television, and now we are getting cable television, satellite television, interactive television, videotelephone, teleconferencing, video-conferencing, videotape, video disk, videotext, teletext, facsimile, electronic mail, computer-aided management systems, computer-telecommunication linkages, and ISDN (Integrated Services Digital Network), *all within one generation.* There simply has not been the time to explore their implementations and assess their impact on doing business, to adapt ways of doing business to them, or to figure out how to best train people in those adaptations. What *is* clear is that the old rules of thumb no longer apply, and we have not *developed* the new one's, much less taught them to anybody. More disturbingly, it is becoming clear that there may not be any rules of thumb anymore.

As implied by these developments in communication technology, task ecologies are changing too fast for rules of thumb to have any useful lifetime. And, of course, such technology is only one of the contributers to our rapidly changing world, organizational, and task ecologies today, The "bottom line" on how to do business most effectively at home may now be the same as it is internationally: *the bottom line is that there is no bottom line.*

Thus we are faced at home today with much of what faces us on an international assignment: rapidly changing organizational and task ecologies. The challenges are the same: cope effectively with the ecoshock brought about by these changes and develop strategies for doing business responsive to them. The most effective strategy is again to develop microcultures tailored to task ecologies. These ecologies consist again of characteristics that are similar across types of organizational change: personnel typically encounter a new organizational culture, tasks tend to be less structured, deadlines or timelines for change are emphasized, and there are problems of communication and support. And they again consist of characteristics that differentiate between them: new workers or management, personnel relocation, new clients or markets, internationalization, new competitors, new organizational structures, new technologies, new regulations, or new products or services. Most organizational change involves a combination of the similarities and some "package" of differences (see Figure 11.2).

Again the skills for developing microcultures are the same, and programs to support the change must be managed. The people who have the skills to be successful internationally are likely to be those who have the skills to be successful in the rapidly changing organizational world at home. That is fortunate since one of the major changes, of course, is the increased internationalization of our organizations and the consequent need for their personnel to move about smoothly and effectively within them.

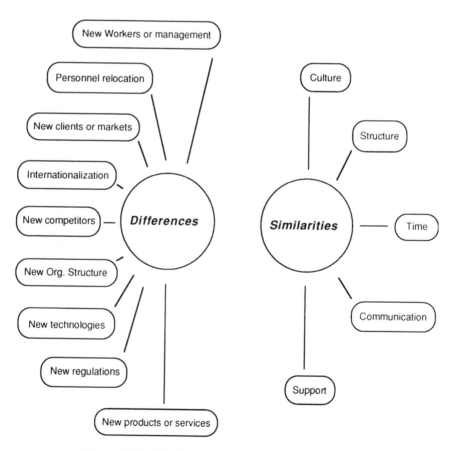

**Figure 11.2**   The Ecology of Organizational Change

# EDUCATION, NOT JUST *MANAGEMENT* OR TRAINING

The point was made in Chapter 8 that building the skills necessary to develop IMCs requires more than training or the other programs alone, but requires that these all be managed. From our own or our organization's perspective of short-term preparation for an international assignment, that theme is appropriate: managing such activities properly will certainly *improve* our chances of doing business successfully. In most instances that is all we and our organization *can* do. However, these skills are not so easily *acquired* in the first place. There is only so much we can do in one month of preparation to modify years of socialization and education.

If we are serious about doing international business, the focus must also be on *education*: high school, undergraduate, graduate, and professional school; in liberal arts, international studies, foreign relations, communication, business, human resources, and management programs. And as demonstrated in this book, that means a lot more than foreign language requirements or area studies. It means developing the curricula that provide our students with the basic skills in how international business is *actually* done successfully: skills that a more focused orientation, training, support, and so forth can sharpen. These skills are quite different from those typically acquired from the highly analytical approach to technical, professional, and management education that is emphasized around the world today.

Further, it appears that a reevaluation of our approaches to education from an international perspective may produce an extra benefit: as just indicated, these same skills are also those required to do business in the rapidly changing ecologies at home as well. So if we are going to be successful in our rapidly changing, international world, then we must turn to *education*, not just management and not just training.

# REDUCING CONFLICT IN INTERNATIONAL BUSINESS

The *Our Way, Their Way,* and *Compromise* strategies for doing business encourage, or even require, the exercise of social power to resolve how it is to be done and thus lead to conflict. This is conflict over and above that produced by differences between participants in the substance of the business at hand: different needs in a treaty or contract negotiation, for instance. Thus the strategy for doing business, itself, may produce sufficient conflict to undermine the success of that business, whatever other difficulties there may be. How many negotiations have failed because the parties could not agree on how to negotiate!

The reason for the conflict is that the more we agree to let them do business *Their Way*, the more we seem to accept implicitly the correctness of their perspective, and the more we may be at a disadvantage skillwise. And, of course, they feel the same about *Our Way*. As first noted in Chapter 2, we take our perceptions of how to do business very seriously: they have taken us as far as we've come, and we don't give them up easily. Thus the danger and depth of conflict when these strategies are used to do business internationally.

Among the other advantages of the IMC strategy is the potential for diffusing that conflict. The crux of the strategy is *not* to focus on whether *Our Way* or *Their Way* is better in any abstract sense, but to focus on the task ecology. The key question becomes: What is the best way for us to do business in this ecology? *The IMC strategy focuses participants away from their conflicting cultures and on the task ecology before them.* A way of doing business is selected because of its appropriateness to the ecology of the particular task; it has no implications for whose way might be better in some other ecology or some different task or better in some abstract sense. Over the latter we fight wars; to do business, we need IMCs.

# INDEX

# A

Academy of Management, 37
Accommodations, 190-94
  airports as, 193-94
  arrangements for, 146
  hotels' role, 191-94
    in doing business effectively,
      192-94
    in coping with ecoshock,
      191-92
  selection of, 190-91
Adams, J. C., 144
Adelman, M. B., 197
Adjustment phases:
  international assignments,
    60-63
  autonomy phase, 63
  contact phase, 61-62
  disintegration phase, 62
  reintegration phase, 62-63
Adler, N., 2, 26, 37, 67
Adler, P. S., 59, 61, 144
Agendas, matching of, 133-34
Airlines, as source of orientation
  information, 160
Airports, as accommodations,
  193-94
Alarm stage, stress, 137
Albert, R., 116, 172
Albrecht, T. L., 197
Alvarez, M. D., 117
American Management
  Association, 37
Anxiety, as ecoshock symptom, 59
Argyle, M., 118
Arpan, J. S., 5
Assignment, definition of, 4
Assignment objectives, as
  organizational support, 195
Assimilators, attribution training
  and, 172-74

Attributions, 116-17
  attribution conflict, 116
  ignorance of attribution conflict,
    116-17
  isomorphic attributions, 116
Attribution training, sense of
  presence training, 172-74
Autonomy phase, of adjustment,
  63

# B

Barna, L. M., 58, 137
Barnett, G. A., 22
Bennett, J., 59
Bennett, J. M., 164
Bennett, M. L., 5, 83
Benson, P. G., 144-45
Berman, M. R., 2, 83, 94-95, 97,
  109-10, 112
Berry, J. W., 23
Bhawuk, D. P. S., 77
Bilateral context, versus
  multilateral context, of
  international assignments, 9
Biological component, of task
  ecology, 49
Blake, R. R., 96
Bochner, S., 57, 61, 69, 123
Body temperature, jet lag's effect
  on, 187
Bond, M. H., 31, 115
Boulton, W. R., 110, 111
Brislin, R. W., 117, 173, 194, 196,
  197
Butler, D., 116-17

# C

Carston, D. E., 182
Castaneda, C., 107, 174

Central cues, ecological
   characteristics as, 110–11
Charge card companies, as source
   of orientation information,
   160
Chesanow, N., 2, 26
Child, J., 37
Christie, B., 136
Circadian rhythms:
   jet lag and, 186–88
   body temperature, 187
   eating/sleeping, 187
   kidney functioning, 187
   liver functioning, 187–88
Cleveland, H., 144
Clothing, 192, 204–5
Cognitive processes, lowered
   effectiveness of, as ecoshock
   symptom, 60
Collen, A., 95
Communication:
   convergence and, 21–22
   difficulties with, 7
Communication skills, 126–36
   agenda matching, 133–34
   development of, 13
   IMCs and, 98
   information exchange, 126–27
   language matching, 128–29
   language training and, 167
   perspective sharing, 130–33
   ritualistic communication,
      129–30
   social influence, 127–28
   symbols, use of, 127–28
   telecommunication technologies,
      135
   training for, 176–77
      key issue, 176
      perception-ecology links, 177
Companionship, as social support,
   198–99
Compatriots, as source of
   orientation information, 160
Compensation, as organiztaional
   support, 196
Competence:
   definition of, 119

negotiating IMCs and, 95
Compromise orientation, 69,
   71–73, 78
Compromise strategy, IMCs and,
   99
Conflict, reduction of, 213–14
Confusian work dynamism, 31
Conrad, C., 17
Contact phase, 61–62
Contrast American episodes, self-
   awareness training and, 172
Convergence:
   of perceptions, 21–22
   communication and, 21–22
Copeland, L., 2, 3, 32, 95, 158,
   194, 197
Coping:
   with ecoshock, 57–66
   with jet lag, 188–90
Coping response, mediation model
   of stress, 179
Cosmopolitan destination, versus
   provincial destination, 10
Cronen, V. E., 22, 125, 131
Cross-cultural approach, to doing
   business internationally, 13
Cross-cultural training programs,
   168
Cues, ecological characteristics as,
   110
Cultural assimilator, 172
"Cultural dominance" orientation,
   67–68
Cultural universals, international
   microcultures (IMCs), 86–87
Culture, 22–37
   definition of, 22–23
   ecological basis, 23–25
   levels of, 25–37
      national culture, 25–31
      organizational culture, 31–37
Culture-general training, 180–81
Culture shock, *See* Ecoshock
Culture-specific training, 180–81
Culture training, 168–80
   communication skills, 176–77
   for sense of presence, 169–74
   for social skills, 175–76

Culture training (cont.)
for stress-management skills,
178-80

**D**

Dawson, J. L. M., 23
Deadlines, 6-7
Depression, as ecoshock symptom,
59
Desatnick, R. L., 2, 5, 83
The desirable, awareness of,
111-14
Dinges, N. G., 67
Diplomatic cultures, *See*
International microcultures
(IMCs)
Disintegration phase, 62
Divergence:
of perceptions, 22
reentry shock and, 65
"Doing business":
definition of, 3
hotels' role in, 192-94
impact of sense of presence on,
107-8
Domestic assignments:
versus international
assignments, 16-38
convergence and
communication, 21-22
culture, 22-37
perception, 17-21
*See also* specific topics
Domestic intercultural
assignments, managing of,
208-10
Donoghue, J., 83
Druckman, D., 96

**E**

Eating:
jeg lag's effect on, 187
coping strategies, 188
Ecological universals, 86
Ecology:
of assigned tasks, 23-24

of international assignments,
6-11
differences, 8-10
similarities, 6-8
task-specific characteristics,
10-11
perception-ecology link, 41-42
perception tailored to, 48
Ecoshock:
coping with, 57-66
hotel's role in, 191-92
cross-cultural training programs
and, 168
definition of, 57-58
IMCs and, 98
lack of social support and, 199
reentry shock, 64
simulation training and, 174
symptoms of, 58-60
Education:
need for, 213
*See also* Training
Empathy, 117-18
definition of, 117
as skill, 118
Establishing contact, developing
social skills for, 205
"Ethnocentric" orientation, 67-68
Exchange role, 15
international assignments, 10
Exhaustion stage, stress, 137
Experiential/simulation training,
sense of presence training,
174

**F**

Face-to-face interaction, versus
mediated interaction, 9, 15
Familiarity, as social support,
197-98
Films, as source of orientation
information, 160
Fontaine, G., 119, 138, 194, 197,
199
Forgas, J. P., 42-44
Fu, M. Y. C., 5
Furnham, A., 57, 123

**G**

General adaptation syndrome
(GAS), 137
imbalances in, 137–38
Generic management srategy,
148–51
Generic problem solving, sense of
presence and, 118–20
Getting role, international
assignments, 10
Giving role, international
assignments, 10
Global organizations, 9
Globerman, S., 2
Goldberg, V., 186, 188
Goldstein, R., 117
Governments, as source of
orientation information, 160
Griggs, L., 2, 3, 32, 95, 158, 194,
197
Gudykunst, W. B., 83
Guidance, as social support, 197

**H**

Hall, E. T., 109, 131
Hammer, M., 83
Handy, Charles, 33–36
Harris, P. R., 2, 26, 32, 157, 194
Harvey, J. H., 117
Hayes, J. L., 37
Heath, C., 193
High-context communication,
131–33
High/low individualism countries,
29
High/low masculinity countries, 30
High/low power-distance bosses,
29
High/low uncertainty-avoidance
countries, 29
Hofstede, Geert, 17, 28–31, 86
Holmes, T. H., 58
Hopmann, P. T., 137
Hosts:
reaction to appearance, 192–93
recognition of jet lag, 190
Hoy, F., 110, 111

Hudson, D. D., 175
Hughes-Wiener, G., 119

**I**

Ignorance of attribution conflict,
116–17
IMC networks, 199–202
functions of, 201–2
members of, 200
personalization provided by,
204–5
where to find, 200–201
Incentives, as organizational
support, 196
Individualism, as work-related
value, 29
In-flight magazines, as source of
orientation information, 159
Information, as social support,
197
Information exchange,
communications and,
126–27
Information sharing, matched
agendas and, 134
Integrated coping response,
179–80
Interaction training, sense of
presence training, 174
Intercultural approach, to doing
business internationally, 13
Intercultural sensitizer, 172
Intercultural training programs,
169
International assignments, 3–5
adjustment phases, 60–63
coping with stress, 138–40
definition of, 4
doing business effectively, 66–77
ecological differences, 8–10
bilateral versus multilateral
context, 9
cosmopolitan versus provincial
destination, 10
face-to-face mediated
interaction, 9
giving versus exchanging
versus getting roles, 10

International assignments (cont.)
    organizational identity, locus
        of, 8-9
    organizational type, 8
    short- versus long-term
        assignments, 9
    technological differences, 10
    ecological similarities, 6-8
    communication, 7
    people, 7
    place, 6
    structure, 8
    support, 7-8
    time, 6-7
    travel, 7
    ecoshock, coping with, 57-60
    impact on personnel adjustment/
        effectiveness, 4-5
    premature return from, 4-5
    reentry, 64-66
    versus domestic assignments,
        16-38
    *See also* Adjustment phases
*The International Assignment,*
    159-60
*The International Business
    Travelers' News,* 159
International cultures, *See*
International microcultures
    (IMCs)
International hotels, role in coping
    with ecoshock, 191
International microcultures
    (IMCs), 74-77, 79-101
    approaches to, 83-85
        expected behaviors, 84-85
        strategic responses, 85
    building of, 12
    business rules of, 82
    characteristics of, 85-93
        lifetime of IMCs, 92-93
        members of IMCs, 193
        task ecology, 86-92
    definition of, 74, 80-81
    development of, 194-97
    quality of, 97-98
    skills in developing IMCs, 98-99
    subjective/psychological
        manifestation of, 82-83
    tasks relevant to, 81-82
International world, 2-3
Interpreters, role of, 167-68
Irritability, as ecoshock symptom,
    59
Isomorphic attributions, 116

**J**

Jain, N. C., 109, 117
Jet lag, 185-90
    circadian rhythms, effect on,
        186-88
    coping with, 188-90
    definition of, 186
Johnson, J. H., 136

**K**

Kealey, D. J., 144, 152
Kelley, H. H., 116-17
Kelley, L., 31
Kidney functions, jet lag's effect
    on, 187
Kincaid, D. L., 22
Kindel, T. I., 84-85
Klemp, G. O., 44
Kohls, L. R., 164
Kraemer, A. J., 172

**L**

Language matching, 128-29
Language training, 166-68
    interpreters, role of, 167-68
Lie, H., 31
Limousines, 193
Liver functions, jet lag's effect on,
    187
Local hotels, role in coping with
    ecoshock, 192
Long-term assignments, versus
    short-term assignments, 9,
    14
Long-term illness, as ecoshock
    symptom, 59
Low-context communication,
    131-33

Low/high individualism countries, 29
Low/high masculinity countries, 30
Low/high power-distance bosses, 29
Low/high uncertainty-avoidance countries, 29

**M**

McCaffery, J. A., 119
McClelland, D. C., 44
Magazines, as source of orientation information, 160
Management:
   of international assignments, 142–51
      generic strategy, 148–51
      management strategy, 146–48
      objectives of, 143–46
Mangone, G. J., 144
Martin, J., 64
Masculinity, as work-related value, 29
Matching agendas, 133–34
Matching language, 129–30, 134
Matching ritual, 129–30, 134
Maynard, W. S., 67
Media, social presence of, 136
Mediated interaction, versus face-to-face interaction, 9, 15
Mediation model of stress, 178–79
Meichenbaum, D., 136
Melatonin, 189
Mental appraisal, mediation model of stress, 179
Michaels, G., 117
Microcultures (MCs), 39–54
   characteristics of, 49–52
   compared to social episodes, 42–44
   perception-ecology link, 41–42
   strategies, 41–47
   task ecology, 40–41
      components of, 49
      exercise, 52
      manipulation of, 52–54
Minors, D. S., 186
Moran, R. T., 2, 26, 33, 157, 194

Motivation, negotiating IMCs and, 95
Mouton, J. S., 96
Mrosovsky, N., 186
Multilateral context, versus bilateral context, of international assignments, 9
Multinational organizations, 9
Mumford, S. J., 133, 152–53, 194
Murray, G., 82, 107

**N**

National culture, 25–31
   exercise, 27–28
   widely shared perceptions, 26–27
   work-related values, 28–31
National organizations, 8–9
The necessary, awareness of, 108–11
Negotiating IMCs, 95–97
Newspapers, as source of orientation information, 160

**O**

Oberg, K., 57
Office services, provided by hotels, 193
Okabe, R., 132
Organizational change, managing of, 210–12
Organizational culture, 31–37
   definition of, 31–32
   perceptions associated with, 32–33
      appearance, 32
      communication, 32
      eating habits, 32
      exercise, 33–37
      management processes, 33
      relationships, 33
      rewards, 32–33
      time, 32
      values/norms, 33
Organizational identity, locus of, 7–8

Organizational libraries, as source of orientation information, 159
Organizational support, 146, 194–97
Organizational types, involving international assignments, 7
Orientation programs, 146, 155–62
    information provided in, 159–60
    role in managing international assignments, 160–62
    traditional approaches, 156–60
Orientations, 66–78
    commonly described orientations, 66–72
    compromise orientation, 69
    "cultural dominance" orientation, 67–68
    "people are the same" orientation, 66–67
    "when in Rome do as the Romans" orientation, 68–69
Ornstein, R. E., 106
Orvis, B. R., 116–17
Ossorio, P., 44
Our Way strategy, 68, 69, 78, 213–14
    IMCs and, 99

**P**

Paranoia, as ecoshock symptom, 59
People:
    cultural differences, 7
    sense of, 108–9
"People are the same" orientation, 66–67
Perception:
    convergence of, 21–22
    culture and, 19
    definition of, 17–21
    doing business and, 20
    ecological basis, appreciation of, 24–25
    exercise, 20–21
    importance of, 18–19
    international microcultures (IMCs) and, 94

perception-ecology link, 41–42
    shared perceptions, 23
    source of, 19
    subjective culture, 19
    tailored to ecology, 48
    widely shared perceptions, 26–27
    zero-sum perceptions, 94–95
Perceptual-motor reactions, reduction of, as ecoshock symptom, 59
Performance appraisal, as organizational support, 196
Periodicals, as source of orientation information, 159
Personnel, impact of international assignments on, 4–5
Perspective sharing, 130–33, 135
    low/high-context communication, 131–33
    purpose of, 130–31
Physical component, of task ecology, 49
Physiological arousal, mediation model of stress, 179
Place:
    psychological differences, 6
    sense of, 108
Porter, R. E., 109, 117
Positive instance bias, 99–100
The possible, awareness of, 111
Posttraining paralysis, 182
Power distance, as work-related value, 29
Practical intelligence, microcultures and, 44
Premature returns, from international assignments, 4–5
Preparation assistance, as organization support, 195
Presence, sense of, *See* Sense of presence
Prolonged stress, 138
Provincial destination, versus cosmopolitan destination, 10
Public libraries, as source of orientation information, 159

**Q**

Quality, IMCs and, 97-98

**R**

Rahe, R. H., 58
Rahim, S. A., 4
Ratliffe, S. A., 175
Raven, B. H., 127
Reentry, 64-66
  assistance in, as organizational
    support, 196-97
  reentry shock, 64
Reintegration phase, 62-63
Resistance stage, stress, 137
Resources, as social support, 197
Ricks, D. A., 5
Rissman, A. K., 182
Ritualistic communication, 129-30
Ruben, B. D., 58, 144, 152

**S**

Salmon, P. A., 186
Samovar, L. A., 109, 117
Sarason, B. R., 136
Sarason, I. G., 136
Screening, 146
  role in managing international
    assignments, 153-54
  screening questions, 153, 154
  traditional approaches to,
    151-53
Scribner, S., 44-46
Seelye, H., 68, 137
Self-awareness training, sense of
    presence training, 172
Self-selection, 146, 154-55
  definition of, 155
Sense of presence, 135
  attributions, 116-17
  definition of, 104-5
  development of, 12-13
  ecological awareness and, 108,
    109
  empathy, 117-18
  generic problem solving, 118-20

IMCs and, 98-99
  impact on doing business, 107-8
  intuitiveness of, 109-10
  need for, 106
  as perceptual skill, 103-8
  stereotyping, 114-16
  training for, 169-74
    attribution training, 172-74
    experiential/simulation
      training, 174
    interaction training, 174
    self-awareness training, 172
    skills developed, 169-70
    techniques, 170-72
    worksheets, 171
Sense of remote presence, 136
Shaefer, S. L., 95
Shared perceptions, 23
Short, J., 136
Short-term assignments, versus
    long-term assignments, 9,
    14
Short-term illness, as ecoshock
    symptom, 59
Shuter, R., 22, 125, 131
*Signature* magazine, 159
Simulation training, sense of
    presence training and, 174
Singer, M. R., 17, 97
Singleton, W. T., 118
Skill:
  definition of, 119
  management requirements,
    37-38
Sleeping:
  jet lag's effect on, 187
  coping strategies, 188-89
Slobodin, L., 182
Smith, R. E., 136, 179
Social component, of task ecology,
    49
Social episodes, compared to
    microcultures (MCs), 42-44
Social influence, communications
    and, 127-28
Social presence, 136
Social skills, 123-26
  development of, 13, 122-23

Social skills (cont.)
  establishing relationships,
    125-26
  generic approach to, 125
  IMCs and, 98
  reduction of, as ecoshock
    symptom, 60
  self-confidence, 125-26
  training for, 175-76
    importance of, 175
    key issue, 175
    strategies, 175-76
Social support, 146, 197-99
  assistance with, as
    organizational support, 197
Status/recognition, as
  organizational support, 195
Steele, Fritz, 47-48, 109, 118, 119,
  203
Stereotyping, 114-16
  determining accuracy of, 115-16
  "exceptions" to, 116
  inaccurate stereotypes, 115
  refinement of, 115-16
Sternberg, R. J., 46-47, 444
Stewart, E. C., 26
Stress:
  alarm stage, 137
  assistance in managing, 196
  coping strategies, 138-40
  definition of, 136
  ecoshock as, 58-59
  exhaustion stage, 137
  general adaptation syndrome
    (GAS), 137-38
  imbalances in, 137-38
  jet lag and, 188-89
  mediation model of, 178-79
  negotiating IMCs and, 96
  prolonged stress, 138
  resistance stage, 137
  travel and, 185
Stress-management skills, 136-40
  development of, 13
  IMCs and, 98-99
  training for, 178-80
    generic approach, 178

  mediation model of stress, 178
Stressors, 136
Stressor situation, mediation
  model of stress, 179
Structure, lack of, on international
  assignments, 8
Subjective culture, 19
Support, 194-206
  developing skills in, 203-4
  development skills, 203-4
  of hotels, 193
  IMC networks, 199-202
  lack of, on international
    assignments, 7-8
  organizational support, 194-97
  relationship to international
    assignments, 199
  social support, 197-99
Support needs, identification of,
  203
Support networks, identification
  of, 203-4
Sussman, N. M., 64
Symbols, use of, in
  communication, 127-28, 129

**T**

Task, sense of, 109
Task ecology:
  international microcultures
    (IMCs), 86-92
  cultural universals, 86-87
  ecological differences, 87-90
  ecological similarities, 86-87
  microcultures (MCs), 40-41
  components of, 49
  exercise, 52
  manipulation of, 52-54
  rapid changing of, 211-12
Task-specific ecological
    characteristics, 10-11
Taxis, 193
Team-building workshops, social
    skills training and, 175
Technical/professional training,
  165-66

Technology, differences in, 10
Telecommunication technologies,
135–36, 211
effective use of, 135–36
Their Way strategy, 68–69, 71–73,
78, 213–14
IMCs and, 99
Third culture perspective, 83
Third cultures, *See* International
microcultures (IMCs)
Time, sense of, 108
Time pressures, on international
assignments, 6–7
Tolerance limits, perceptions and,
21–22
Training, 5, 146, 163–83
communication skills, 176–77
key issue, 176
perception-ecology links, 177
culture-general training, 180–81
culture-specific training, 180–81
culture training, 168–80
communication skills, 176–77
for sense of presence, 169–74
for social skills, 175–76
for stress-management skills,
178–80
duration of, 181
function of, 164
how provided, 181
for international assignments,
lack of, 5
language training, 166–68
posttraining paralysis, 182
sense of presence, 169–74
attribution training, 172–74
experiential/simulation
training, 174
interaction training, 174
self-awareness training, 172
skills developed, 169–70
techniques, 170–72
worksheets, 171
technical/professional training,
165–66
training programs, 164
when given, 182

where given, 181–82
who should provide, 181
who should receive, 181
Travel, 185–90
arrangements for, 146
increase in international travel,
3–4
jet lag, 185–90
coping with, 188–90
definition of, 186
preparation assistance, 195
stress associated with, 7
Travel agents, as source of
orientation information, 160
Travel dysrhythmia, *See* Jet lag
Triandis, H. C., 17, 19, 116, 182

**U**

Uncertainty avoidance, as work-
related value, 29
Understanding, provided by
support systems, 205
University libraries, as source of
orientation information, 159
Useem, J., 83
Useem, R., 83

**V**

Visitors, as source of orientation
information, 160
Vulnerability, feelings of, as
ecoshock symptom, 60

**W**

Wagner, R. K., 44, 46–47
Wasilewski, J., 68
Waterhouse, J. M., 186
Wedemeyer, D. J., 4
Weldon, D. E., 182
Wells, G. C., 117
Whatley, A., 31, 37
"When in Rome do as the
Romans" orientation, 68–69

Williams, E., 136
Winham, G. R., 2
Wiseman, R. L., 83
Worksheets, sense of presence
    training, 171
Worthley, R., 31

**Z**

Zartman, I. W., 2, 83, 94–95, 97,
    109–10, 112
Zero-sum perceptions, 94–95